JUST GOOD
BUSINESS

JUST GOOD BUSINESS

The Strategic Guide to Aligning
CORPORATE RESPONSIBILITY
and **BRAND**

Kellie A. McElhaney, Ph.D.

Berrett–Koehler Publishers, Inc.
San Francisco
a BK Business book

Berrett-Koehler Publishers, Inc.
235 Montgomery Street, Suite 650
San Francisco, CA 94104-2916
Tel: (415) 288-0260   Fax: (415) 362-2512   www.bkconnection.com

Ordering Information

Quantity sales. Special discounts are available on quantity purchases by corporations, associations, and others. For details, contact the "Special Sales Department" at the Berrett-Koehler address above.

Individual sales. Berrett-Koehler publications are available through most bookstores. They can also be ordered directly from Berrett-Koehler: Tel: (800) 929-2929; Fax: (802) 864-7626; www.bkconnection.com

Orders for college textbook/course adoption use. Please contact Berrett-Koehler: Tel: (800) 929-2929; Fax: (802) 864-7626.

Orders by U.S. trade bookstores and wholesalers. Please contact Ingram Publisher Services, Tel: (800) 509-4887; Fax: (800) 838-1149; E-mail: customer.service@ingrampublisherservices .com; or visit www.ingrampublisherservices.com/Ordering for details about electronic ordering.

Berrett-Koehler and the BK logo are registered trademarks of Berrett-Koehler Publishers, Inc.

Printed in the United States of America

Berrett-Koehler books are printed on long-lasting acid-free paper. When it is available, we choose paper that has been manufactured by environmentally responsible processes. These may include using trees grown in sustainable forests, incorporating recycled paper, minimizing chlorine in bleaching, or recycling the energy produced at the paper mill.

Library of Congress Cataloging-in-Publication Data
  McElhaney, Kellie A., 1966–
  Just good business : the strategic guide to aligning corporate responsibility and brand / Kellie A. McElhaney.
    p. cm.
  Includes bibliographical references and index.
  ISBN 978-1-57675-441-2 (hardcover : alk. paper) 1. Social responsibility of business.
  2. Brand name products. I. Title.
  HD60.M378 2008
  658.4'08—dc22   2008036675

First Edition
14 13 12 11 10 09   10 9 8 7 6 5 4 3 2 1

Book design and production: BookMatters; copyediting: Mike Mollett; proofreading: Anne Smith; indexing: Gerald Ravenswaay

This book is dedicated to my two daughters, Isabel and Juliana, who gave me the best job ever—being their mother. I feel most proud of my work when answering their "What do you do, Mommy?" questions. Keep being lionesses and telling us to turn off the water while we are brushing our teeth, to stop taking so many napkins, to buy a hybrid car, to recycle. You are our future, thankfully, and we should all refuse to destroy it for you.

This book is also dedicated to Mike Homer, a mentor, a friend, a hero, and a truly great man. I am indebted to him.

Contents

Preface
It's Time to Take the Next Step

Our society will be remembered not only for what we create,
but also for what we refuse to destroy.
—John Sawhill, environmentalist

I have been teaching, researching, running programs and centers, advising on company projects, consulting, and speaking globally on corporate social responsibility (CSR) since 1993. It has been a wild ride, through a field that started in relative anonymity, marginality, and insignificance and has moved fairly rapidly to front-page news. Indeed, the *Wall Street Journal* in 2006 and again in 2007 included CSR as one of the areas—along with finance, marketing, accounting, and operations—that it assessed in its annual rankings of top business schools.

In 2008, the venerable *Financial Times* added CSR to its global MBA rankings (I might add that our Center for Responsible Business at the Haas School of Business at the University of California at Berkeley was number one!). CSR has been the main theme of the World Economic Forum at Davos, Switzerland, at several of the annual meetings, including in 2008, when Bill Gates spoke of the need for more "creative capitalism—an approach where governments, nonprofits, and businesses work together to stretch the reach of market forces so that more people can make a profit, or gain recognition, doing work that eases the world's inequities."

And finally, after years of calling it misguided, misaligned, illegal, and useless, the *Economist* admits that "CSR, done well, is just good business and is here to stay." To that I say amen.

I have observed and investigated the trends of analysis in CSR and have witnessed firsthand a dramatic change. Discussions have moved from asking why CSR, to measuring the impact of CSR, to developing strategic CSR frameworks, and finally to talking about, communicating, marketing, and branding a company's CSR strategy. Throughout all of these trends and discussions, I have not felt compelled to write a book—until now. Telling a company's CSR story, after it has developed significant CSR substance and strategy, has never been more powerful than it is today. Integrating a company's CSR into its brand is even more powerful—not only for consumers but for employees, suppliers, partners, retailers, and investors alike.

In the pages that follow, I will invite and encourage you to take the next step in the evolution of CSR. We are now at a turning point in the evolution of CSR, and it's time to go beyond the question of whether or not it is the right thing to do. For an increasing number of companies, there is no question that adopting a CSR strategy is the right thing to do—they are doing it. And not just to be green or to be better corporate citizens or to improve their image. They are doing it because of the positive impact CSR has on employee recruiting, loyalty, and retention; on differentiation in the marketplace; on customer loyalty and attraction—and on the bottom line.

A lot of CSR is out there in the business world, but not a lot of it is effective, strategic, high-impact CSR. By the time you finish reading this book, you'll understand that creating a CSR strategy and a CSR program is only half the job. The other half is creating your CSR story and branding, and publicizing it regularly and widely. Of the effective, strategic CSR that is out there in the business world, very little of it is effectively communicated. With this book you have all the tools you'll need to do all that and more. Now it's your turn. I hope that someday I'll have the opportunity to write about your own successful CSR efforts.

Finally, I believe that corporate responsibility, along with being just good business, can also help to provide and repair something that is desperately lacking in our world today: hope. *Let us refuse to destroy HOPE. Corporate responsibility builds hope.*

PART I

Corporate Social Responsibility— Just Good Business

Part I discusses the current state of the art of corporate social responsibility (CSR)—what it is, why companies should integrate it into their business strategies, and why they should do it now. You will learn how to develop effective CSR strategies, how to align your company's core objectives, competencies, and stakeholder expectations, and how to maximize CSR's value within the firm.

Introduction

WHY CSR? WHY NOW?

> How wonderful it is that nobody need wait a single moment before starting to improve the world.
>
> —Anne Frank

If you doubt the impact that corporate responsibility strategy—even if incremental—can have on a big business's bottom line, consider the example of vending machines at Wal-Mart. After receiving employer-provided training on sustainability, Darrell Meyers, an associate (employee) in a North Carolina Wal-Mart store submitted a suggestion to remove light bulbs from the company's vending machines. Removing the light bulbs—which stayed lit 24/7 and needed to be replaced from time to time by maintenance workers—would help prevent wasting energy while saving the company money. As it turned out, Darrell's thinking was right on target. When his idea percolated up to Wal-Mart's corporate headquarters in Bentonville, Arkansas, someone ran the numbers and estimated that Darrell's suggestion would save the company more than $1 million a year.

Guess what? You'll be hard pressed today to find a vending machine in any Wal-Mart store or office anywhere that has a functioning light bulb in it.

This book is about corporate strategy and corporate social responsibility (CSR) and how you can leverage the power of branding and communication to ensure that your company's CSR efforts are noticed by the public, including customers, sponsors, partners, suppliers, employees, and shareholders. Remember: a lot of CSR is out there in the business world, but not a lot of it is effective CSR. And even of the limited amount of effective CSR strategy that exists, no company has yet captured the market on effectively communicating it in such a way as to maximize business value. Most companies are scared to death to communicate their CSR.

In fact, many companies have been and are doing more—not less—in the world today to improve education, health care, and environmental protection, to name but a few key areas of social focus. The problem, however, is that they are not talking about it, and they are not telling their stories when recruiting new employees, branding new and existing products, or entering new markets. The result is that the average consumer, employee, government regulator, or supplier has no idea what if anything the company is doing when it comes to corporate social responsibility. They therefore cannot factor the company's CSR efforts into their choices when deciding what product to buy, where to work, or how to invest.

If this book has power, it is in convincing you that you can and should brand and communicate your CSR. Corporate social responsibility can help firms—particularly those in highly commoditized industry segments such as consumer products or banking and financial services—to differentiate their brand and stand out above the noise when price, quality, and convenience are relatively equal. This positive impact creates a competitive advantage for these firms both when markets are up and when they're down.

However, you cannot move to branding your company's CSR until you first agree on a definition of CSR and name it and second—and perhaps more importantly—develop an integrated CSR strategy with substance and business impact.

Exactly What Is CSR and What Should You Call It?

Unsurprisingly for a field that was catapulted so quickly from irrelevance to center stage, there is scant understanding of and agreement on what CSR is—and what it is not. CSR might simply be defined as "using the power of business to create a better world" (the definition offered by the global leadership network Net Impact). In my own work, I think of CSR in terms of corporate strategy, and I advocate that firms use CSR as part of their portfolio of business strategies. To that end, since 1998—and for the purposes of this book—I have developed and use the following definition of *strategic corporate social responsibility*: a business strategy that is integrated with core business objectives and core competencies of the firm and from the outset is designed to create business value and positive social change, and is embedded in day-to-day business culture and operations.

The lack of a be-all and end-all definition of corporate social responsibility is no excuse for a company not to engage in CSR. Companies must consider the definitions given here—and others—and then quickly start by defining the term for themselves. If CSR is to be treated as a part of an effective corporate strategy, then its definition would be, by definition, unique to each firm based on that company's objectives, risks, opportunities, and competencies. In my experience, this is most definitely the case.

One challenge to nailing down a definition of CSR within organizations is that the concept of corporate social responsibility itself goes by many different names. What is called *corporate social responsibility* in one organization might be given the label *spiritual capitalism* in another. Below is a list of the most common labels used by companies in referring to the things they do involving CSR:

- corporate responsibility
- sustainable development
- sustainability
- environment, social, and governance (ESG)
- social enterprise
- global citizenship
- corporate citizenship
- values-driven business
- natural capitalism
- spiritual capitalism
- compassionate capitalism
- people, planet, profits

I personally try to dissuade leaders from wasting a lot of time deciding on a name for their own CSR efforts. I advocate only that they indeed call it *something*, give it a name and use it consistently; that they define it for themselves as a company; and that they develop and execute a business strategy around the name, communicate it, and brand it.

As you read through the chapters that follow, please keep the strategic aspect of corporate social responsibility in mind. To me, this is ultimately what gives CSR its power to not only change the world for the better but to improve the company's bottom line. An effective CSR strategy can do all that while enhancing employee loyalty, productivity, and retention; while granting a company license to operate in new countries and markets; while giving a product or service a competitive advantage; and while giving a company a sticky brand story to tell in the marketplace. If you don't demand that both your CSR goals and your financial goals be achieved in parallel and together, then your corporate social responsibility program will likely be unsustainable in the long run. As soon as you have a down quarter, your CSR resources will be the first to be cut.

Why CSR Now?

I used to stay awake at night wondering if CSR was really as mainstreamed in the wide world as it was in my professional life. As someone who specializes in the field, it's easy to mistakenly believe that the entire world revolves around the object of my professional affection. That feeling grew particularly nagging when I moved to Berkeley, as so many things that are top of mind in Berkeley (tree sitters trying to keep a football field from being expanded is just one recent example) rarely hit the rest of the world's screen of top priorities. I knew from my voracious bedtime reading (that is, nonacademic reading) that issues of corporate responsibility graced every major magazine cover in this country during the course of 2007, and have continued to do so in 2008.

But it wasn't until I accidentally picked up an issue of a particular magazine one day that I become 100 percent convinced that CSR's time had finally come and that it had hit the mainstream. Why was I so convinced?

Because the magazine in question—*Sports Illustrated*—is a venerated mainstream magazine that featured CSR, more specifically global warming, on its cover in March 2007.

If the sports fans of the world were now getting CSR—and getting it in a way that truly mattered to them—then CSR was finally entering the mainstream of American thought. The *Sports Illustrated* feature highlighted the most popular and spectacular baseball parks in the United States, predicting that if global warming continues at its current pace half of them would be underwater and rendered obsolete by 2050.[1] The issue also discussed Babe Ruth's famous slugging and predicted that if he had been playing today at the same strength as he did when he was alive, Ruth would not have hit nearly as many home runs due to higher levels of particulates in the air resulting from the degradation of our environment. *Sports Illustrated* brilliantly stuck close to its core competency— sports—while making CSR and climate change relevant to its athletics-loving readers.

A number of key factors have come together in the past few years, causing the idea of corporate social responsibility to explode and finally make its way into mainstream business thinking:

- The impact of technology that gives citizens immediate access to transparent information and news at the click of a computer key or press of a cell phone button
- Nongovernmental organizations' (NGOs') increasing sophistication in targeting corporate malfeasance
- The shifting of resources and power away from governments and the public sector and toward the private sector
- Workers demanding that their employers contribute to bettering the world
- Pockets of consumer pressure
- Generation Y (aka Millennials) proving to be the most cause-focused generation in decades

But of all the reasons, perhaps the single most important driver of CSR today is the expectations-reality gap. As Figure 1 indicates, the public's

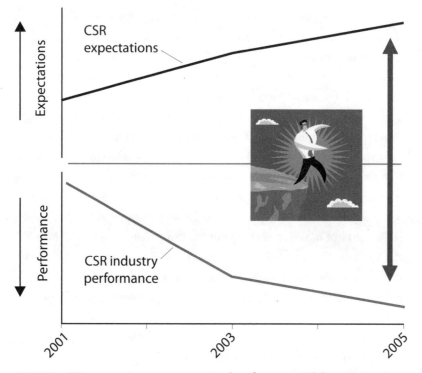

FIGURE 1. CSR expectations versus perceived performance (Globescan, 2005)

current expectation that business *will* operate in society's best interests has rapidly increased to an all-time high, while the public's perception that business *is* operating in society's best interests has rapidly declined to an all-time low. This gap is leading to an increasingly perilous erosion of trust in business.

Across various surveys that are conducted annually, business is typically last or second to last among most-trusted institutions to operate in society's best interests, depending on what is happening in government that day.

Part of the challenge in this expectations gap arises because of the difference between *perception* and *reality*. To bridge this image-identity gap, companies must constantly work to build their CSR results, substance, and initiatives into internal and external brand stories.

Self-Assessing Your CSR

Most companies are already engaging in CSR at some level. To develop an effective CSR strategy, you need to know where your company stands in the process. This requires self-assessment. Simon Zadek of AccountAbility—an international nonprofit organization that promotes accountability for sustainable development—discusses five stages that companies generally pass through when engaging in CSR.[2] (See Figure 2.)

Stage 1: Most companies enter the CSR space as a *defensive* move, because somebody (employees, media, NGOs, government) has exposed poor behavior or practices and has pushed the company to improve. Think Nike when the company was exposed in 1998 for various human rights abuses in its Asian factories.

Stage 2: With the pressure on, company leaders know they need to do something to *comply*—preferably in a way that requires the minimum investment of precious financial resources while demonstrating to critics that the company is taking action to address their concerns. An example of this step is when every apparel company, in an effort not to be the next Nike, developed a supplier code of conduct and sent placards spelling out the code (in English, mostly to non-English-speaking countries) to every factory from which they sourced,

Stage 3: Ultimately, the company develops some sort of *management* process or system (for example, the ISO 14000 environmental management standards) so that responsibilities can be assigned internally, the actions can be measured, and they get done. But as with most things that are risk mitigating, these activities tend to be viewed as a *cost* to the company, not a *value* or *opportunity*. And without looking at CSR as value creating, innovation or creativity are lacking in the CSR activities.

Stage 4: Companies view CSR as part of their value- and opportunity-creating *strategies*, on par with their business development, research and development, branding, and market-entry strategies. Indeed, the trend is finally changing with CSR. When General Electric launched its

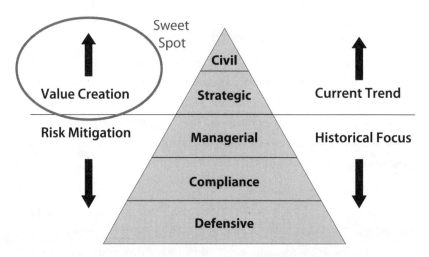

FIGURE 2. Stages of CSR (Adapted by permission from Simon Zadek, *The Civil Corporation: The New Economy of Corporate Citizenship* [Sterling, VA: Earthscan, 2001], chapter 6).

Ecomagination program in 2006, it did so unabashedly with the view that this was going to become a value-creating strategy for the firm:

> Ecomagination puts into practice GE's belief that financial and environmental performance can work together to drive company growth, while taking on some of the world's biggest challenges. [Ecomagination is] about the GE commitment to products and services that are as economically advantageous as they are ecologically sound.[3]

GE is a great example of a company that finally views CSR as part of its business strategy—to sell more goods and services and create value for the firm. The Ecomagination program meets my own definition of CSR, as it also exists to create positive environmental value by focusing on increasing energy efficiency. Ideally, as more and more companies begin to view CSR as a business strategy—and succeed in creating value, including increased sales, entry into new markets, and brand differentiation—their competitors will follow suit and even collaborate, raising the entire civil foundation.

I argue that some of the best, most strategic CSR has been executed by firms that entered the CSR spectrum from a point of significant public pain: consider Nike and sweatshop allegations or GE and effluent dumping in the Hudson River. As it is for humans, pain (and the compelling desire to avoid it) can be a particularly effective motivator for businesses. So I tend not to get caught up in why a company was originally motivated to engage in CSR. For me, the ends justify the means, and even coming at CSR from a defensive or self-serving motivation does not take away from the resulting positive environmental and/or social contributions.

Stage 5: The final stage in the CSR maturity process is when the company changes the rules of the game, raises the *civil* foundation, and indelibly changes society.

A company at the highest stage of corporate social responsibility embeds CSR into its daily business operations, collaborates with other companies, and attempts to change the rules of the game or attack a problem or social issue at its cause. A good example of this is Product Red, styled as (PRODUCT)[RED], a brand collaborative that is licensed to American Express (United Kingdom only), Converse, Gap, Emporio Armani, Motorola, Apple, Hallmark Cards, Dell, and Microsoft. The idea is for a percentage of the profits of Red products to be sent directly to the Global Fund to Fight AIDS, Tuberculosis, and Malaria.

In this case, Gap reaches Zadek's stage 5, or civil stage, most profoundly in that not only does a percentage of the sales of the company's Product Red products go to the Global Fund, but it also tries to source the materials for these Product Red products from AIDS-, malaria-, and tuberculosis-ridden countries such as Lesotho to create economic development. Along with its Lesotho sourcing program, Gap has committed to support women, children, education, and health care in Lesotho. This is an example of Gap going deeper than simply a cause-marketing program but further integrating Product Red into its supply chain and sourcing strategy.

Why Now?—the Value of CSR

There has been much debate, disagreement, and discussion about the value of corporate social responsibility to the bottom line, as well as the constant search for the holy grail—a study that will directly and causally link CSR to an exact increase in share price. Unfortunately, this study does not and likely never will exist. The linkage of corporate social responsibility practices to increases in earnings has thus far proved to be indirect and correlational at best.

The best evidence for the financial benefits of effective strategic CSR can be found in the areas of human resources, reputation, branding, and operational cost savings. For example, employees are significantly interested in, more highly satisfied with, and more loyal to companies that have a proven commitment to corporate responsibility. Therefore, CSR can be used as an effective strategy to recruit and retain top talent, a fact that has obvious positive implications for the bottom line. This strategy will be especially important as baby boomers leave the workforce in increasing numbers and a smaller pool of Millennials rises to take their place.

CSR can help firms to differentiate their brand and stand out above the noise in industries such as consumer products or banking and financial services where price, quality, and convenience are relatively equal. Particular demographics of consumers have proved their willingness to spend more, remain loyal, and prefer brands that support a cause or an issue about which they care deeply. And replacing high-wattage incandescent light bulbs with low-wattage, more energy-efficient fluorescent light bulbs; changing water fixtures to slow flow; and changing photocopiers to double-sided will decrease operating costs.

Like Wal-Mart, plenty of companies are doing things that are good for both the environment and the bottom line. But in order to recognize many of the business benefits of CSR, they have to strategically communicate their CSR efforts to employees, consumers, governments, business partners, and suppliers. To date, few firms have been aggressive or successful in building CSR into their brand, or in treating it as a viable sub-brand. This, I believe, is a grave error. But it is an error that can be righted by making CSR a vital part of a company's strategy. The next chapter talks about how to do just that.

1

BUILDING YOUR
CSR BUSINESS STRATEGY

Strategy without tactics is the slowest route to victory.
Tactics without strategy is the noise before defeat.
—Sun Tzu

In honor of Earth Month, Wal-Mart launched its first-ever in-store *maga-logue* (kind of a cross between a magazine and a catalogue), which aimed to inform its customers—roughly 200 million of them in a month—on actions they could take, while shopping at Wal-Mart, to help the planet. This was great business strategy not only for Wal-Mart in promoting the greenness of its own brand but also for General Electric, Procter & Gamble, Horizon Organic, and Clorox—all of whose environmentally friendly products are given premium promotional space in the maga-logue, not to mention premium in-store shelf space.

As we have already seen, CSR is quickly gaining corporate mindshare—an increasing number of companies in almost every industry are adopt-ing CSR principles and initiating CSR programs. The realization that com-panies can and should play an important role in their communities—and across the nation and around the world—while making a profit is quite a step up from the old belief that the sole purpose of companies is to increase value for shareholders.

Today, many businesses are taking the next step in the evolution of CSR in business. Many business leaders are realizing that CSR is also a viable component of their overall business strategy, along with such traditional functions as marketing, branding, research and development, innovation,

A budget-friendly guide
to helping the planet.

WAL★MART
Save money. Live better.™

walmart.com/green

WAL★MART
Save money. Live better.™

(Wal-Mart, *Earth Month*,
April 2008)

Sure, an electric car can help
the environment. But so can
a shopping cart.

Of all the ways to help the planet, the most beneficial might just
involve the things we do every day — like how we shop. You see,
simple choices in what we buy and use can have a positive impact
on the world around us. And when you're part of 200 million
Wal-Mart shoppers, those simple choices can add up to some
amazing things. Like preventing enough CO_2 emissions to equal
taking over 11 million cars off the road, just by changing a light bulb.

So take a look inside. You'll find products that'll help save you
money while helping the planet as well. You'll also see how you
multiplied by 200 million can equal a brighter future for us all.

YOU x 200 million = A brighter future

talent management, and operations. They are therefore beginning to
accord CSR strategy the same level of attention they give to these other
vital corporate functions and, better yet, weave their CSR strategies in
with their branding, marketing, and operations.

That is good news, indeed, because *strategic* corporate social responsibility executed well is *effective* corporate social responsibility.

A Typical Corporate Goal

Management guru Peter Drucker perhaps said it best: "What gets planned gets done." Companies have long known that to achieve their goals, they need strategies that get everyone within the organization headed in the right direction at the right time, and that ensure that resources are mobilized where required.

For example, consider a typical corporate strategy—in this case one from Hewlett-Packard (HP) in 2006 to "Establish HP as the world's leading information technology company."

> HP's goal is clear and is likely to be inspirational to the company's employees: to establish Hewlett-Packard as the world's leading information technology company. Just as clear are HP's three interdependent strategies for achieving this goal: targeted growth, capital strategy, and efficiency. If you are an HP employee, you know that if you contribute to one or more of these three strategies, you are helping the company achieve its greater goal of information technology supremacy. Moreover, as an employee you know that your performance will be measured on your success in contributing to one or more of these strategies.

So far, so good. At least until we come to the typical company's CSR goals.

Because they know that they need strategies to achieve their mainline business goals (such as HP's goal to become the world's leading information technology company), many companies also know that they need to develop strategies for their corporate social responsibility goals as well. However, because the goals for most CSR efforts aren't in support of typical corporate functions such as marketing, manufacturing, sales, and so forth, many companies are unsure of what goals to set for CSR efforts or what strategies to pursue. The result is often a hodgepodge of unfocused, unconnected, and unrelated strategies in search of an overarching goal.

Although perhaps a bit extreme, Figure 3 does demonstrate elements of the typical CSR strategies that you're likely to find in most businesses today.

Which approach do you think will be more effective: one like HP's

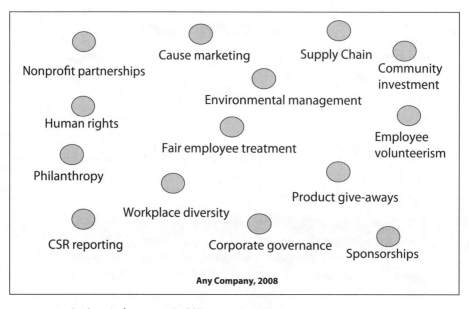

FIGURE 3. A typical company's CSR strategies

tightly focused goal to become the world's leading information technology company or the scattershot—and all-too-typical—CSR strategies illustrated in Figure 3?

The Case for a CSR Goal

Business leaders are beginning to realize that an effective corporate social responsibility goal can be much more than a feel-good public relations (PR) release for prospective customers, employees, shareholders, and other stakeholders; it can have a significant and positive impact on the bottom line.

The IBM Institute for Business Value recently surveyed a group of 250 business leaders worldwide and found that more than two-thirds (68 percent) are focusing on corporate social responsibility activities to create new revenue streams. In addition, more than half (54 percent) of the surveyed business leaders believe that their companies' CSR activities are already giving them an advantage over their top competitors. According to IBM's report on these findings, "When aligned with business objectives, companies are beginning to see that CSR can bring competitive differentiation, permission to enter new markets, and favorable positioning in the talent wars."[4]

In a landmark *Harvard Business Review* article, Michael Porter and Mark Kramer proposed a new way to look at the relationship between business and society, a way that unifies company philanthropy with the management of CSR efforts and embeds a social dimension in their core value proposition. According to Porter and Kramer,

> The fact is, the prevailing approaches to CSR are so fragmented and so disconnected from business and strategy as to obscure many of the greatest opportunities for companies to benefit society. If, instead, corporations were to analyze their prospects for social responsibility using the same frameworks that guide their core business choices, they would discover that CSR can be much more than a cost, a constraint, or a charitable deed—it can be a source of opportunity, innovation, and competitive advantage.[5]

Shift of Power and Resources

Corporations wield tremendous power today, in large part because of the often quite significant financial impacts that they have on the communities, states, and countries where they have their offices, factories, and manufacturing plants and where they do business. As corporations have grown in size and financial power, the balance of power of resources in the world has changed as well. If you doubt that this is indeed the case, a quick look at the 2006 list of top one hundred economies in the world (as measured by gross domestic product [GDP]) should change your mind (see Figure 4).

One has to look only to number twenty-two before a corporation appears on this list. Exxon Mobil and Wal-Mart have higher gross domestic products (GDPs) than 75 percent of the world's countries! Exxon Mobil made more money in 2007 than any corporation has in history. Imagine the positive impact that these companies could have on the world, especially if their efforts were focused and strategic instead of scattershot and random. Clearly, if we want to change the world, we'll need companies

TOP 100 WORLD ECONOMIES

Rank	Company/Country	GDP (World Bank) [millions, USD]
1	United States	13,201,819
2	Japan	4,340,133
3	Germany	2,906,681
4	People's Republic of China	2,668,071
5	United Kingdom	2,345,015
. . . .	. . . .	. . . .
22	Wal-Mart Stores	351,139
23	Exxon Mobil	347,254
24	Poland	338,733
25	Austria	322,444
26	Royal Dutch Shell	318,845
27	Norway	310,960
28	Saudi Arabia	309,778

FIGURE 4. Top economies of the world, 2006 (Revenue from *Fortune* magazine; GDP from the World Bank).

like Exxon Mobil and Wal-Mart with their power, reach, and resources on board.

The good news is that increasingly we do have the power, reach, and resources of companies like Wal-Mart, as well as thousands of other businesses, on board. Indeed, corporate social responsibility programs and initiatives are rapidly proliferating.

The bad news is that despite this plethora of CSR programs, most corporate efforts to date have been neither strategic nor well communicated. To be effective in their CSR efforts—and to reap all the potential benefits— these companies will need to do more than simply doing good in their communities. They will also need to approach CSR strategically, as a viable component of their overall business strategy, along with marketing, branding, research and development, innovation, talent management, and operations. And they will need to effectively tell their CSR stories.

Developing an Effective CSR Strategy

At a minimum, companies should focus on the following set of good practices as they craft their own CSR goals.

Senior leadership and management of the firm, including the board of directors, must make an authentic, firm, and public commitment to CSR efforts, and engage with them. Often CSR efforts will be born organically throughout lower levels of employees. But even if they are, at some stage senior executives have to be brought on board, have to commit to them, and have to engage with them. This clear vision of CSR needs to be embedded within the core values of the firm and reflect those values, and it must be linked to the mission, vision, and values of the organization. And this core vision needs to openly recognize that CSR is central to creating not only social or environmental value but also to creating business value. Firms must be unabashedly unapologetic about that. CSR efforts should be treated and managed as core business strategy, just as are the strategies of marketing, research and development, capital expenditure, and talent management.

Determine the top three business objectives of the company and develop CSR goals that will contribute to the achievement of those business objectives. In developing CSR goals the company must determine what its business objectives are. Defining business objectives is not as easy an exercise as it might appear to be at first glance. Often when five business managers from the same firm are asked to describe their business objectives and priorities, they give five different answers. For example, I worked with a tech company in Silicon Valley whose top executive quickly answered the top three business objectives question: "Growth, growth, and growth." Her human resources director looked quite pained in responding that until they were able to rein in the company's high turnover rate, they were going to have a difficult time growing, growing, growing.

A CEO might say that the most pressing objective is to increase market share or increase sales, while the human resources leader might say that it is to recruit and attract the best talent, engage and unify disparate employee silos and business units, or improve employee satisfaction. The conversation needs to happen at a deeper level so that the CSR goals can serve these general objectives. Is the objective to grow in new markets? If so, which ones? Is it to penetrate new customer segments or grab market share from competitors? If so, which market segments?

After business objectives are determined, align CSR goals with the firm's core competencies. This practice requires focus and discipline. Typically CSR is executed in an ad hoc, nonintegrated fashion. CSR initiatives can originate in all parts of an organization and if mapped are often not linked to what the firm actually knows, does, or is expert in. CSR can come from the passion of a CEO (or historically from his wife) or a motivated employee. It can come simply from the causes and issues whose representative organizations (often nonprofits) ask the firm for support. Firms should, however, seek causes and social or environmental strategies for which they own part of the solution.

The classic case is Ford Motor Company Fund's support for breast cancer research—to the tune of $95 million over fourteen years to Susan G. Komen for the Cure. There is no argument that this is an eminently worthy cause that meets a significant need, and it is only one of many programs that Ford supports in its CSR effort. But it is an important part of Ford's CSR effort, and there is no strategic link between the company's support for breast cancer research and the building of cars and trucks. Automotive companies know cars, transportation engineering, and design, so perhaps support for alternatively fueled vehicles and addressing the global and environmental challenges around gasoline dependency are more fitting to the firm's core competencies and business objectives of selling more cars. Not only may Ford be in a better market position if it focuses on more strategically aligned causes, but the results of its initiatives in these areas may lead to the development of innovative new automotive technologies, which will lead to new products and revenue streams.

Fully integrate CSR efforts into the governance of the company and into existing management systems. If CSR efforts are not built into the performance appraisal system for a company's employees, for example, then the chances are good that they will not be fully embraced and executed with the precision of the commonly measured functions such as sales and staff management.

You should view CSR as both a risk-mitigation strategy and an opportunity-seeking strategy. Seek to find the sweet spot, that is, the intersection between business and social or environmental returns. Seek out partners in the community who have developed deep expertise in the cause or issue you are targeting, and work with these organizations, usually in the nonprofit sector, to develop the best solution and build capacity. Nonprofit partners are also in a better position to help the company communicate its CSR efforts, as nonprofits enjoy a higher level of trust.

Finally, develop clear performance metrics, or key performance indicators, to measure the impact of your CSR efforts. These metrics should be both internal (measuring reputation, market share, brand perception, sales, operating expenses, and employee satisfaction) and external (measuring achievements in society and the environment). If no performance metrics are in place, you will have no way to prove that the effort was effective, and it will not be sustainable over the long haul.

The CSR Maturation Process

CSR can also be seen as a maturation process inside of an organization. Historically, companies have viewed their CSR commitments through a philanthropic lens—they are spending some of their profits in the community to garner positive PR and customer goodwill. The level of engagement in the philanthropic model is actually quite low, however, because the effort is not built into the companies' day-to-day operations or management systems. Such efforts are typically handled as completely separate functions, divorced from profit and loss responsibility, and they are typically not integrated into business objectives or core competencies.

In fact, many CEOs are offended when pressed on the idea that their philanthropic endeavors should result in any business value whatsoever. These leaders do good works simply because it is the right thing to do, or they do it to recognize tax advantages—a one-time strategy. However, as companies begin to move their CSR efforts from simple philanthropy or

Growth stage:	Philanthropic	Transactional	Integrative
Level of engagement	Low	———→	High
Importance to mission	Peripheral	———→	Strategic
Magnitude of resources	Small	———→	Big
Scope of activities	Narrow	———→	Broad
Interaction level	Simple	———→	Intensive
Managerial complexity	Infrequent	———→	Complex
Strategic value	Modest	———→	Major
EXAMPLES ACTIONS:	• Donation • Grants	• Event sponsorship • Cause-related marketing • Employee volunteerism	• Joint-advocacy • Joint-action • Deep partnerships • Financing principles • Changing rules of industry

FIGURE 5. The CSR maturation process

public relations, they move into transactional and then integrative phases in their maturation process, with the characteristics shown in Figure 5.

When working with a company to develop its CSR strategy, I first ask senior management what their goals are for their CSR effort. Do they simply want to run a good business? If so, they would want a strategy of undertaking ad hoc initiatives—like recycling or donation matching—brought to them by their employees from time to time. Do they simply want to give back to their local communities and be a good neighbor? If so, they would want a strategy of creating partnerships with local charities, such as supporting local schools, arts organizations, or hospitals. Do they want to be a beacon for other leaders and transform their entire industry? Then they would want a strategy of developing industry collaboratives and consistently communicating what they are doing so as to lead their peers.

Howard Schultz, of Starbucks and his fair trade pricing, and John Mackey, of Whole Foods and his emphasis on natural and organic foods, are great examples of leaders whose companies have become beacons. It would be difficult to argue against the fact that these leaders started industry trends toward increasing fair trade and organic offerings. Ironically, most CEOs and senior leaders like the idea of leading their industries, yet

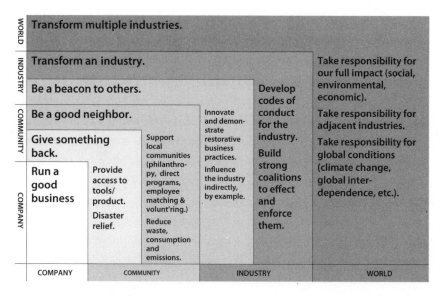

FIGURE 6. A CSR landscape

their CSR programs do not match these desires. Most corporate CSR falls into the category of being a good neighbor and simply giving back to the community. Giving back to the community is not a bad or inadequate endeavor. But the firm's CSR strategy should match the space in which the senior management says they want to play.

Figure 6 illustrates the levels of CSR, from having an impact on the company by helping run a good business to having an impact on the world by transforming multiple industries.

Aligning Core Objectives and Competencies

To be effective, CSR goals must be aligned with two things:

- Core business objectives
- Core competencies of the firm

The first step for a company is to align its CSR goals with its specific business objectives for a particular time period. Aligning CSR goals with business objectives is not as easy an exercise as it may appear. Although there may be many legitimate business objectives, to develop the most efficient and successful CSR goals, the company must prioritize its primary objectives for the time frame. Business objectives can and should change over time, and they should be routinely reexamined in relation to the CSR strategy.

Aligning CSR strategy with the firm's core competencies is the next step for creating effective fit with CSR initiatives. This step requires focus and discipline. But regardless of the amount of effort involved, the time spent will be worth it. Creating a CSR strategy will unify your efforts, giving them much more power than if they remain a random mishmash of disparate initiatives. And once your CSR strategy is in place, you'll be able to move to the next step: leveraging the power of branding your CSR—the topic of the next chapter.

Chapter 2

CAPTURING THE POWER OF BRANDING

Brand is everything, the stuff you want to communicate to consumers and the stuff you communicate despite yourself.

David F. D'Alessandro, *Brand Warfare*

One Saturday afternoon my two daughters, ages six and eight, had a conversation that illustrates the power of CSR messaging.

"You only need one napkin, Juliana. Don't you know what napkins are made of?" Isabel, the eight-year-old asked. Juliana remained completely uninterested, true to her six-year-old self. "Napkins are made of paper. And do you know where paper comes from?" Isabel pressed on. "Paper comes from trees. And do you know what lives in trees? Animals live in trees."

At this point, Juliana, who adores animals, houses snails in her underwear drawer, and has already proclaimed her future career as an animal doctor, became engaged. "Yeah, I know there are many animals that live in trees. Squirrels live in trees, and birdies, and tree frogs."

Isabel's voice got higher. "They have to cut down lots of trees to make paper to make those napkins," pointed out Isabel. Quivering voice and big eyes ensued. "And when they keep cutting down those trees to make those napkins, the animals lose their homes." Tears appeared in Juliana's eyes.

"Then where do the animals go?" she asked.

"They try to go to other trees, but then those trees get cut down, too," continued Isabel. "And then the animals have nowhere to live." Instantly, both were crying uncontrollably as Juliana quickly shoved the four or five napkins she had grabbed back into the holder.

I gave them both hugs and told Isabel how very proud I was of her, not

FIGURE 7. Sign in Dreyer's Ice Cream Shop, Oakland, California

only for knowing that this was so but for teaching this valuable lesson to her little sister. "Where did you learn this?" I asked her, expecting to be fully credited. "Well, Mommy, last night Bobbie's daddy took her and me to Dreyer's after soccer practice to get ice cream. There was this sign on each table that said, 'Only one napkin per customer, please.' And below the sign, some kid had drawn a picture of trees with happy animals living in them. I asked the ice cream shop owner what the sign meant, and he told me, and he also told me that local elementary school children had made the signs for him as part of a class project." (See Figure 7.)

As the air quickly leaked out of my expanded ego, I was struck by two thoughts. First, it was not my brilliance at all that had made this socially responsible impact on my eldest child, and now on my youngest child. Second, the power that companies can have to influence people—if they so choose—can be profoundly positive.

The Power of Communicating CSR

This scenario is but one example of the power of communicating one shop owner's corporate social responsibility initiative. But what's particularly interesting about this example is that it was decidedly low budget and low tech. This was not one of those $1 million advertising campaigns twelve months in the making with complex messaging delivered through multiple brand channels. This campaign did not originate with an enlightened CEO who hired a team of CSR consultants to develop an in-depth CSR strategic plan for the firm. This was not an edict that came down to all Dreyer's ice cream shop franchise owners from the European headquarters of the parent company, Nestlé. This was a simple but, as it turned out, powerful transfer of hope from a fourth-grade daughter to her ice-cream-shop-owning father that rippled out to two second-grade girls and a dad, and from there to a younger sister and a mom, and likely to many other customers who patronize that Dreyer's store.

This scenario shows the power that a small, low-cost, low-tech message can have on the world. Now imagine the impact if Nestlé were to communicate a well-developed CSR strategy—one pillar of which is *protecting the environment*—through its Dreyer's brand in much the same way, but on a scale many magnitudes larger. The potential impact on Nestlé's brand could be significant. We already buy Dreyer's ice cream exclusively in our household, as instructed by my daughters. However, perhaps a more profound result is that to this day Isabel monitors the paper usage of anyone who enters our home—all because of that one-time interaction with Nestlé, an $80-billion-a-year global business giant.

Consider the possibilities if this company had strategically intended to communicate this brand message.

You Cannot Not Communicate

Humans communicate, both verbally and nonverbally, with others around them almost constantly. Even not saying anything can be a message. And because companies are populated by and run by humans, they too communicate, continually and in many different ways. The question is not whether we communicate (we do) but instead *how well* we communicate.

Corporate executives I talk with—everyone from CEOs to vice presidents of corporate communications to brand managers to directors of corporate responsibility—list the myriad reasons, risks, and fears they have about publicly communicating their companies' work in the area of corporate social responsibility. Convincing these gun-shy corporate leaders to begin to tell their CSR story can be a real and ongoing challenge.

You cannot not communicate.

As obvious as this concept is, when it comes to CSR, few business leaders embrace it. It seems that the more in-depth, mature, and advanced the firm's CSR strategy and substance, the less likely the world is to know about it—even when the company already expends millions on branding and messaging its products and services.

This is a significant lost opportunity.

Once a firm has developed, executed, and integrated a CSR initiative, branding it can be an innovative and valuable business strategy to reach multiple critical constituencies—employees, suppliers, business partners, investors, peers, and consumers—inside and outside of the corporation. However, like anything else in business, to be effective the branding has to be done right.

CSR Substance First, Branding Second

Any company that is serious about branding its CSR must first develop deep, strategic CSR content. In today's world of high expectations for companies, increasing demand for transparency, and immediate access to information through technology, branding CSR without substance is a sure recipe for disaster.

I cannot emphasize this point enough: CSR substance first, branding second.

That is not to say that companies need to keep quiet about it while they are developing their CSR strategy. In fact, transparently communicating the status of CSR strategy development is justified, at least at the beginning. Strategic CSR is a process, not a destination, so waiting until

You really can't not communicate. Even if you choose not to tout your admirable efforts in doing socially responsible business, plenty of others (bloggers, magazine writers, newspaper reporters, television correspondents, and more) will, whether you like it or not. In 2008 *Condé Nast Portfolio* magazine published its list of the Green Eleven—companies that the magazine says are some of America's most eco-savvy corporations. Landing on this particular list would certainly be a feather in the cap of any CEO.

However, *Portfolio* also compiled a list of ten companies that should be doing better in their corporate social responsibility efforts, out of concern "that many corporate environmental efforts may be degenerating into self-serving marketing stunts." The CEOs of these companies might not be quite as happy.

Three Companies from *Portfolio*'s Green Eleven

- **Bank of America.** Its internal recycling program saves the equivalent of more than 200,000 trees a year, and it offers employees who buy hybrid cars a $3,000 cash-back incentive.

- **Wal-Mart.** The former bane of the green movement now has one of the most ambitious environmental plans of any U.S. company: a proposal to power every store with 100 percent renewable energy.

- **Starbucks.** Its "bean-to-cup" approach creates eco-accountability at every stage of its supply chain, with recycled-paper sleeves alone saving the equivalent of 78,000 trees in 2006.[6]

Three Companies from *Portfolio*'s Toxic Ten

- **Apple.** Significant amounts of phthalate, a toxin thought to cause birth defects, have been found in the iPhone and iPod headphone cords.

- **Cargill.** A Cargill plant in Virginia has been putting out effluents that are overwhelming wastewater treatment facilities, causing the dumping of toxic substances into the North Fork Shenandoah River.

- **Alcoa.** Alcoa's aluminum smelters release 6.1 million pounds of air pollution annually.[7]

the CSR strategy is complete before communicating it would be unwise. Branding, too, is an ongoing strategic process.

My recommendation is for the two strategic processes to be done in tandem and in alignment with one another. Although cynics will assume that I am persuading companies to brand their good works out of self-serving motivation, the fact is that even the companies with the most strategic CSR initiatives, with measured impact and significant results, are paralyzed by fear of communicating any of their CSR achievements.

The ABCs of Branding

From the corporate perspective, one of the most frustrating things about brands is that one can never wholly own a brand, only try to manage it, because it exists primarily in the eye of the beholder. In fact, since each person has her own brand and reputation perspective, a brand can have literally millions of perceptions and interpretations attached to it.

Primarily, a brand is a promise to deliver on and reinforce people's perceptions. The ideal story arc of the brand promise works like this:

- The consumer begins with general awareness. "Have we met somewhere before?"
- She then learns about the brand attributes and points of parity and differentiation. "What makes your brand different? Why shouldn't I just buy the cheaper generic version? What will this brand do for me?"
- She will then experience a feeling about the brand and render judgment. "Is it good quality? How does it make me feel?"
- Finally, she builds a relationship with the brand. She could develop loyalty and feel a sense of attachment with the brand. "This brand understands me. I can relate to this brand."

As you can imagine, there are practically unlimited opportunities for this ideal story arc to go wrong. Strong brands set out to deliver on a promise, and they make it happen. Weak brands fail to deliver.

People develop perceptions of a brand by instinctively aggregating every single interaction they have with the brand, from the wonderful last product they bought to the time one of the products broke, from the unsubstantiated rumor they read on an Internet blog to the story they heard from a friend who works for the company, and from the rude customer service agent they got on the phone to the unusually friendly salesperson.

Marketers call these events *touchpoints.* Even if a company focuses on a few touchpoints, it cannot control the multitude of external forces the brand is subject to. Thus, brand managers can only anticipate the needs, set the stage, and hope all the pieces fall into place.

Keep in mind that brands are not just aimed at consumers anymore. Think of branding as a broad strategic management tool. Brands can affect the type of talent you are able to recruit to your firm as well as how your current employees perform, whether activists decide to publicly and ardently boycott your firm, what fund analysts write in their reports about your firm's value, what the government decides to regulate, and how easily your firm is able to enter new countries and new markets.

Thinking of branding to various stakeholders in comparison to a stakeholder engagement approach, which is a common CSR framework, is helpful for thinking about brand audiences. We can look at it briefly through the eyes of the company Brown-Forman. (See Figure 8.)

Brown-Forman is the parent company of Jack Daniel's whiskey, Fetzer wine, and more than twenty other spirits and wine brands. For Brown-Forman, the primary CSR issue is obvious: alcohol abuse. It is what I refer to as the company's "scariest question," which is what its CSR strategy should focus on if it is to be perceived as authentic and credible. What is the company's responsibility for the fact that it makes products that can be fine when used in moderation but can lead to tragic consequences when abused? Where does Brown-Forman's responsibility begin and end? To answer the question, Rob Frederick, Brown-Forman's director of corporate responsibility (and a former MBA student of mine), started by looking at the wide variety of groups that have some stake in what the company does. Consumers are only one part of the mix. When Frederick evaluates a strategic corporate social responsibility decision, he can focus on these groups to identify which stakeholders have the biggest stake in the issue and to define their interests.

Branding works the same way. Each of these stakeholders (or audi-

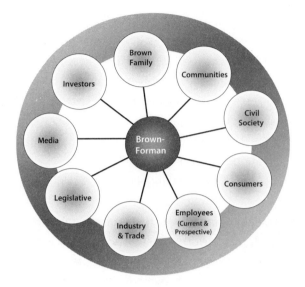

FIGURE 8. Stakeholder engagement at Brown-Forman (Courtesy of Brown-Forman).

ences) has a perception of the Brown-Forman brand. In fact, for a corporate parent like Brown-Forman, where most consumers don't even know the company exists, other audiences are much more important.

After a career of helping major corporations develop CSR management strategies, I noticed that my clients were terrified of communicating their accomplishments. I was confused. If you have something worthwhile to say—something you are proud of—then why wouldn't you want to talk about it? But at the same time, I understand that when you stick your neck out, you are more likely to get your head chopped off.

So I started to think about why companies communicate anything at all and looked at the things that make great brands great. I found a striking overlap between branding drivers and what a strong CSR strategy can help achieve.

In Brand We Trust

Trust is a valued commodity among institutions in our society. You can't buy trust. You can only earn it over a relatively long time. Unfortunately,

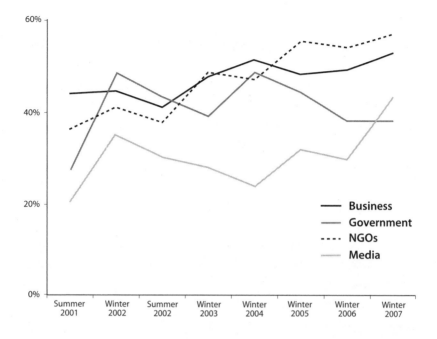

The State of Trust (Edelman)

FIGURE 9. The state of trust in institutions in the United States (Edelman, *2006 Annual Edelman Trust Barometer*, http://www.edelman.com/trust/2008/prior/2006/ FullSupplement_final.pdf).

you can lose trust over an extremely short time. So it makes sense to build some trust to store up in your bank in case you find yourself in a position in which you need to draw upon it.

Recognizing the business implications, the public relations firm Edelman has been tracking trust for eight years. Edelman has found that over the past three years, nonprofit organizations have been the most trusted entity. Interestingly, government has plummeted, a reaction likely caused by issues like the Iraq war, weapons of mass destruction, and so forth. Business and the media have been able to fill this void and improve their trust standing over the same period.[8] (See Figure 9.)

Nevertheless, many people simply do not trust communications from companies, regardless of the vehicle, be it an advertisement, a press release, an annual report, a Web site, or even a speech by the CEO. They need to hear the message from someone they trust before they will believe it.

People just trust great brands. This trust is based on the idea of brand promise, the belief that a company can deliver on expectations. It drives business tangibles like sales, investor relations, and recruitment and business intangibles like corporate reputation and approval by regulatory authorities, the license to operate.

Edelman's research indicates that trust matters. When U.S. and European Union (EU) citizens distrust a company, they will refuse to buy its products or services, refuse to invest in it, refuse to work for it, and—of most concern—criticize it to people they know. Ignore corporate trust at your own peril! You may have a negative viral marketing campaign on your hands.

Just ask General Motors. GM launched an innovative user-generated viral initiative that allowed people to create their own GM television commercial using technology on GM's Web site. Before the company knew what was happening, hundreds of new commercials were being created ridiculing the company for its record on environmental sustainability.

Brands' Reputation

Jeff Bezos, founder and CEO of Amazon.com, said, "reputation is what people say about you after you have left the room." Corporate reputation is not much different.

Harris Interactive, a prominent market research firm, conducts an annual survey called the Reputation Quotient. The Reputation Quotient is a fascinating attempt to quantify something as intangible as brand. Why would the firm try? Why should companies care? Because there is ample agreement that intangibles such as brand contribute to more of a firm's financial value than ever before. Some estimates indicate that as high as 80 percent of a firm's value comes from intangibles such as brand.[9] The survey rates the companies on twenty attributes in the following six categories: financial performance, social responsibility, workplace environment, quality of products and services, vision and leadership, and emotional appeal.

As you might imagine, of the six sets of attributes that make up the Reputation Quotient, emotional appeal has the highest predictive ability of brand reputation. Do consumers admire, trust, and respect your brand and feel good about it and themselves when they buy it? The attribute with the second-highest predictive ability is the quality of your goods and services: do they work well?

Social responsibility is the third-ranking attribute on predictive ability of reputation. However, when you rank the six attributes by what consumers know about a company, CSR is dead last.[10] That is, when consumers go about formulating their perspective on the reputation of a brand, they tend to know most about the brand's emotional appeal, related to the product or service itself. So social responsibility is the third-highest attribute in its ability to predict reputation, but it is the attribute about which consumers know the least. This is a significant missed opportunity and one that I think firms that have CSR substance can easily capture.

In the 2006 Harris Interactive reputation rankings, Microsoft surprisingly edged out Johnson & Johnson, "whose emotionally appealing baby-products business had kept it in first place for a remarkable seven consecutive years." The *Wall Street Journal* attributed Microsoft's jump to Bill Gates's significant personal philanthropy through the Bill and Melinda Gates Foundation, which is entirely separate from Microsoft the company.

"The involvement of Bill Gates and his wife in their charitable foundation has had a definite impact on Microsoft's reputation," explained one survey respondent. "It's hard to separate Bill Gates' image from that of Microsoft; to me, they're one and the same."[11]

This reaction is classic example of branding. Anything Bill Gates does is inexorably linked to the Microsoft brand. In fact, Microsoft's corporate philanthropy efforts are far less impressive and lower impact than are Gates's.

But it's not a causal relationship. Researchers have found that having a "poor corporate reputation makes building strong brands difficult, but a good reputation is no guarantee of success."[12] In other words, good corporate reputation is not necessarily a point of parity for strong brands, partly because consumers are more likely to know about poor reputations than good ones so are more likely to punish poor reputations than they are to reward good ones.

Working for a Winning Team

Strong brands build loyalty, not just with consumers but also with employees. People want to build relationships with strong brands. They want to give them their business, and they want to work for the winning team.

More often than not, companies with great brands will say their most important asset is their people. After all, brands without a brand manager will likely whither and die. Companies cannot rest on their laurels in today's marketplace.

Research conducted by the Great Place to Work Institute shows that companies that invest in their employees "enjoy higher levels of customer satisfaction and customer loyalty." They also "receive more qualified job applications for open positions, experience a lower level of turnover, and foster greater innovation, creativity and risk taking."[13]

It's no coincidence that these great brands also outperform their peers on the stock market. A stock index of *Fortune* magazine's one hundred best companies to work for has beaten the Standard & Poor's 500 Index over the past eight years.[14]

Building employee loyalty is critical for brands because employees are the best brand ambassadors. Employees need to understand and identify with the brand to sell it. If the rank and file don't understand the brand, how can you expect outsiders to understand it? And your employees are often the only people a consumer will ever interact with in connection with the brand.

CSR Can Be a Method of Keeping Your Brand Relevant

CSR involves some fundamental steps, tools, and processes, as will be discussed in Part II. One of these steps is deep engagement with external stakeholders, such as governments, new markets, future employees, critics, activists, and NGOs. One of the biggest benefits from this stakeholder dialogue and engagement is exposure to future trends, opportunities, risks, and market information.

If Ford Motor Company had been engaging extensively with activist groups rather than focusing on Susan G. Komen for the Cure in the 1990s, it might be further along on hybrid and alternative fuel vehicles than it is today. In short, truly treating CSR as a business strategy, seeking new knowledge, engaging, listening, and using this information to inform business strategy can serve to keep your brand relevant to the themes and trends of today as well as the future. Society and the environment surrounding it will always be relevant, so weave societal expectations into your brand—as long as those expectations and needs fit your core competencies and business objectives.

CSR Branding Can Attract Certain Sought-After Market Segments

Certain stakeholder groups are more ready for CSR messaging than others. Your CSR branding will resonate more highly with some segments than others, so use it accordingly. Happily, these CSR-ready stakeholder groups also happen to be highly sought-after segments. Women, who control over 80 percent of the purchasing power, are receptive to CSR substance and messaging.[15] And this receptiveness applies not only to women as consumers but perhaps equally importantly to women as employees.

Though the extent is contested, the number of women in mainstream business as managers and leaders has been dwindling. Females are certainly still the minority in the ranks of MBA education. Savvy companies can use their CSR substance as a hook with which to engage, attract, and retain top female talent in their employment ranks. Many women are also socially responsible investors, so you can brand your CSR to investors as a method to increase access to capital.

Other sought-after market segments—including Millennials (the generation born between 1978 and 2000); the lesbian, gay, bisexual, and transgender (LGBT) markets; and Hispanics/Latinos—have also proved to be open to CSR messaging. All of these segments can be extremely valuable to your business as potential employees, consumers, suppliers, retailers, and investors. Attract them with your CSR substance and branding. Communicate your CSR authentically and clearly to them, and they will come.

PART II

Connecting CSR Strategy and Brand— Seven Rules of the Road

So far, we've explored why you should take the next step beyond simply doing something good called CSR—the step of turning it into a key corporate strategy, aligned with your core objectives and competencies. We've also explored the power of branding your CSR efforts by communicating those efforts to customers, vendors, shareholders, and other stakeholders and closely linking them to your products and services.

In Part II, we will consider how to leverage the power of branding your CSR efforts, and we will explore a framework of seven principles for effective CSR branding: know thyself, get a good fit, be consistent, simplify, work from the inside out, know your customer, and tell your story.

3

KNOW THYSELF

Self-knowledge is the beginning of self-improvement.
—Baltasar Gracián

In March 2008 the Ford Motor Company announced that it would double its contribution to Susan G. Komen for the Cure each time it sold a Warriors in Pink trim package for the 2009 Ford Mustang. Available in three colors—black, silver, and white—only one thousand of the cars were to be produced for sale. Buyers were able to choose between coupe and convertible models, and the Warriors in Pink Mustangs included a pink ribbon and pony fender badge, pink Mustang rocker tape striping, charcoal leather seats with pink stitching, aluminum-spoke steering wheel with pink stitching and charcoal floor mats with pink ribbon and contrast stitching (that's a lot of pink!).

The Ford Motor Company has been building automobiles since 1903. As of March 2008 the company had sent Susan G. Komen for the Cure more than $95 million in cash and in-kind contributions for breast cancer education and research during the course of its fourteen-year commitment to the organization. Said Connie Fontaine, Ford's manager of Experiential Marketing, "Thanks to the tremendous response from our dealers and customers to the 2008 Warriors in Pink Mustang, we knew we needed to continue offering the package, and we're happy to be able to increase our support for the Cure at the same time."[16]

It sounds like the ideal match: big, beefy Ford Mustang muscle cars and pink-beribboned breast cancer crusaders. Or does it?

Although the fight against breast cancer is inarguably a noble cause—after all, more than 178,000 U.S. women contracted the disease in 2007, and more than 40,000 U.S. women die from the disease each year[17] —the question is this: do Ford's contributions to this particular charity feel out of sync with the business goals and competencies of the company? In Ford's 2007 annual report, president and CEO Alan Mulally states that the company's number one goal is "to build products that are immensely desirable so that we can grow profitably."[18]

What do the Warriors in Pink Mustang and fourteen years of donations to Susan G. Komen for the Cure have to do with achieving Ford's goal of building immensely desirable products and growing profitably? Recall from the introduction that to be an effective business strategy, CSR must be tied to business objectives of the firm. Unfortunately, in the Ford and Susan G. Komen case, I'm not sure of the fit—and I'm not sure that its customers will see it either.

Discovering What Makes You You

In writing this book my goal was not to tell you how to force your CSR efforts to be more authentic. My goal was actually to help you develop a CSR strategy that will be naturally authentic because it is linked to your company's mission, vision, and values. If your CSR strategy is linked to your core competencies, and if it is linked to your business objectives, then it *will* be authentic. The public is not stupid. People understand that a company's primary objective is to create and protect wealth. Almost everything that a company does is linked in some way to creating wealth, and if the company ceases to create and protect wealth, no matter how socially responsible it is, it ceases to be a company and will eventually go out of business.

Another goal of this book is to help companies more effectively tell their CSR stories and link CSR to brand. However, to adequately tell your story and leverage the power of branding your corporate social responsibility, you must first get clarity about what your company is all about and what its core objectives and competencies are.

Much inauthentic, ineffective CSR activity is out there, CSR that exists solely because someone in marketing thought it was time to tap into the rising wave of green consumerism, or because some nonprofit conducted a campaign against the company's labor practices in Southeast Asia, or because the CEO's wife sits on the board for a pediatric AIDS foundation, or for any number of other reactive reasons. Again, people aren't stupid: they know when they are being sold a bill of goods. Greenwashing—painting your company with a thin patina of social responsibility that is easily scraped off upon closer examination—is getting attention by increasing numbers of individuals (many with access to YouTube), watchdog groups, and organizations. If you're not telling the *right* story, then your customers, employees, shareholders, and other stakeholders are going to start wondering why the story you're telling doesn't mesh with their own perceptions of what kind of company you are. The result? The story will lose its effectiveness, and confusion, loss of focus, and loss of business opportunities—not to mention resources spent ineffectively—will follow.

Let's return for a moment to Ford Motor Company's commitment to Susan B. Komen for the Cure. What is the business linkage between this massive automobile manufacturer and the search for a cure for breast cancer, besides the female models so prominently displayed along with the company's vehicles at auto shows all around the world? What is Ford's primary business objective? To design better vehicles and to sell more cars and trucks. It's hard to find the linkage between that particular business objective and breast cancer.

And if you look at Ford's core competency, it's the design, manufacture, and delivery of vehicles, not finding the cure for breast cancer. In short, Ford's partnership with Susan B. Komen for the Cure demonstrates a significant lack of fit between the company and the cause. Ford did not select an issue for which it owns part of the solution. Seeking a cure for breast cancer is clearly a worthy cause—no one would argue that there is not a need for breast cancer research. However, if Ford's management really went through the exercise of CSR strategy development and understood what the company's mission, vision, and values were, they would discover that those values really have nothing to do with health care or breasts but a lot to do with developing the automotive technologies to capitalize on affordable and sustainable new fuels and helping its consumers save money at the gas pump—something that many consumers are concerned with today.

Coincidentally, research indicates that consumers are far less skeptical of a company that integrates its brands with corporate social respon-sibility for which it can see a good fit.[19] So to maximize both social or environmental impact and business impact, it's clearly in the interest of companies to closely align their CSR with their vision, mission, objec-tives, and competencies—to align their CSR strategy with their business. When you take this approach, you'll tap deeper into your existing base of customers, allowing you to transmit your message efficiently and quickly. Not only that, but your customers will tend to become believers in your message rather than skeptics—potentially becoming loyal brand ambas-sadors in the process—and you strengthen your message both internally and externally. These brand ambassadors can help bring you new seg-ments of consumers, penetrate new markets, and win more business.

Dove's Campaign for Real Beauty

On November 29, 2004, Unilever kicked off a global marketing campaign for its Dove soap brand. Called the Campaign for Real Beauty, it turned the advertising world upside down.[20] The marketing campaign—which would include print ads, outdoor billboards, a dedicated Web site,[21] an e-mail newsletter, online viral marketing channels using short films, and more—was different from other campaigns. Instead of using industry-standard thin, young, and unapproachably beautiful female models, Dove chose to use nonmodels, that is, women who looked like the major-ity of its customers—freckled, curvy, older, plus-size, silver-haired, and even wrinkled real women.

Dove started by selecting a social issue—relating to girls and women, their self-esteem, and definitions of beauty—for which it owned part of the solution. In developing its Campaign for Real Beauty, management took a careful look at what Dove was—both the good and the bad—its values, and what they might possibly want it to be in the future. Dove owned part of the problem because—before it launched its Campaign for Real Beauty—it helped contribute to the distorted view of beauty that many people have today. But it also owned part of the solution because it sells beauty and health care products. The company knows exactly what it can—and can't—do.

Unilever, the company that owns Dove, recognized that one of its core competencies was the ability to establish strong brands. Strong brands are developed based on reams of research and analysis. So in capitalizing on this competency for its CSR strategy, Dove spent months researching how societies in its markets across the globe define beauty. It researched the prevailing concepts of beauty and how those concepts contributed to self-esteem, or lack thereof, in young girls and women. Because Dove is a global company, it examined definitions of beauty in the United States, in Europe, in Saudi Arabia, and in India.

When I talk to companies about first knowing what they can and can't do, I focus on getting them to home in on their business objectives. The answer is always to sell more widgets or to sell more services, but I push them to go beyond the easy answer and to look at business objectives two through five, because those tend to tell me more about the pain they are feeling at the moment.

Ask: What Do You Do?

Much of knowing your company begins by simply talking about what it is that your company currently does—what is it known for? When I work with companies, I always have them think in terms of the question everyone gets at a cocktail party—"So, what do you do?"—and I ask them to really think about what their answer is. If you worked for eBay, you might say, "I connect buyers with sellers," or you might say, "I create markets." If you worked for Unilever, you might say, "I sell deodorant and soap," or, "I help to redefine the perception of beauty across the world." Which answer makes you feel more proud of your company and your work? When you start digging deep into what your company is really all about, always ask two questions: What do you do? and What *could* you do? Unilever and its Dove brand clearly asked both of those questions.

Start at the Top

Who should be a part of this initial process of self-discovery? To be effective, you'll need all of your company's major functions represented, ideally by those who make decisions about them and run them. In most cases, this will be your business unit leaders, which means getting participation as high up in the company as possible.

When I worked with eBay to help develop its CSR program, we had the head of human resources, the head of communications, the head of strategy, and the head of strategic partnerships and growth at the table. Often a company will exclude these line functions from CSR planning meetings and instead bring forward its head of community affairs or the head of its company foundation or philanthropic organization. Although they are important, these functions aren't what makes eBay tick (that is, the profit centers). What makes eBay tick are sales, markets, and all of the market segments (cars, jewelry, furniture, and so forth). You want to get people at the table who are responsible for the profit side of the company, not just the cost side. You need strategists and decision makers around the table.

When I work with companies, I ask people where they see the biggest barriers in the company in launching a CSR strategy, and I ask that they bring a few of the people from these areas to the table (not too many at first or they will squelch creativity and brainstorming). Start by brainstorming the set of CSR possibilities that come to the forefront, and then evaluate from there.

I used to try to bring the chief financial officer to the table, but I found that doing so tends to constrain the initial work of the group, as does inviting the company's legal counsel. When you have legal and finance in the room, you can't brainstorm the loudest possibilities because they are trained to talk about the ten reasons why you *can't* do something—not the ten reasons why things will work. The best time to bring in these individuals is after the brainstorming piece is complete and the company has homed in on a strategic direction linked to business objectives and competencies.

Whoever Shows Up

CSR activity often originates with one or two low-level employees in the company who have passion for a cause, and you want to have a blend of participation by both high- and low-level employees. One of those change agents is Barbara Waugh, who works at Hewlett-Packard and who coauthored a book with Margot Silk Forrest called *The Soul in the Computer*, which is about change management, in the context of CSR. The book isn't just about CSR content and substance but is about how to effectively create change inside of a company. Waugh talks about how when she was trying to create change at HP, originally related to domestic partner benefits and diversity, she knew she needed the top executives at the table. They're the ones who make decisions and control who gets the financial and human resources.

Having the decision makers is important, but at some stage you've also got to play with whoever shows up. Understand that your first pass at putting together a CSR program may not include all of your company's top executives. But if you can get just two or three or four of them in the room, and then play with whoever else shows up, you'll get your CSR efforts off the ground and moving forward. And if you're creating positive social or environmental change, and are linked to business objectives, more executives will want to show up.

One strategy I particularly like is to start with the highest-ranking person I can find in the company who will engage in the CSR effort. Then we sit down and decide whom we need to have at the CSR strategy-development table, whom would we like to have at the table, and whom we can get at the table. We make a list, and I ask that person to be the internal champion to go out and bring the people we need to the table. I know from experience that CSR is like a drug—once they get there, people tend to get engaged and stay, particularly if they are taking part in developing the company's CSR strategy.

You Need a Plan

You need to have a plan, a strategy. If your strategy is linked to your core competency, to your business objectives, to your mission, vision, and values, people don't necessarily need to know the end result. They just need to see how it fits into your overall business strategy and to see some clear goals.

For example, at the beginning of Ford Motor Company's CSR development, the company's chairman, William Clay Ford Jr., admitted that Ford had a problem: its primary profit-producing product was fuel inefficient and was not safe. In essence, he said, "It is our biggest profit-making product, but we have a problem. We don't know exactly how we are going to do it, but we know that we need to work on it. We know we need to reduce emissions. We know we need to increase fuel efficiency. We know we need to improve safety. We don't have all the answers, but we have a plan of how we are going to start to move there in the next five years."

That approach worked well for Ford when William Clay Ford Jr. laid it out. The NGO community, which had waged countless campaigns against Ford, was unusually forgiving. The problem is that Ford never communicated the message after that, it did not weave this aspect of its business strategy into its overall business strategy, and it didn't produce, at least not in a way that allowed it to remain competitive with automakers with greater foresight. Perhaps a reason why there was little or no follow-through was because it didn't have a true CSR plan.

If you tie CSR to your business objectives, then it can't go away because it's linked to sales or growth or employee satisfaction or brand loyalty. Companies make a big mistake with their CSR efforts when they don't build a sustainable strategy that is tied to the business objectives of the company. The CSR initiative won't get cut during budget season—as often does philanthropy that's disconnected from cause-related branding—if it's actually contributing to the success of the company on some level.

Another mistake companies make is that they don't work the CSR effort throughout the company. I always advocate having a CSR council—a cross-functional committee that not only comes together to help develop CSR strategy and so feels ownership over it but also is responsible for going back and selling this CSR strategy in members' respective business units. You don't want to keep the CSR marginalized in a CSR department—you want to develop champions throughout the company.

The more you start tying CSR initiatives to the success of the firm, the more a firm starts attaching its CSR to its brand, the less likely it is to go away, because expectations are ratcheted up, not only by employees but by consumers, suppliers, and shareholders. Expectations are high for companies you'd expect, like Whole Foods, Starbucks, Method Products, and Stonyfield Farm. Expectations are also becoming tied to some unlikely companies and brands, including Dove and even Wal-Mart.

Dealing with Cynics

I don't usually deal with cynics in the beginning stages of a new CSR project, but I do eventually try to invite them in. Why? Because cynics are usually nothing more than frightened or wounded idealists who wish they could play. First, you don't want only the choir of believers at the CSR table. Cynics or naysayers often ask good questions that you should consider, particularly when you're developing an effective business strategy. Once you have a good sense of the direction of your strategy, then you invite the cynics in to help you develop it. If you can engage them (and CSR is one of the most engaging business strategies out there) and get them involved, you've won. It's much more difficult for cynics and naysayers to pooh-pooh what they sat at the table and helped to develop.

Ebay

When you have five senior leaders in a room, and you ask the question "What are your business objectives?" you'll often get five different answers. For the sales team it's always "sell more." For the CEO it's always "grow." This was the case at eBay when I started to work with the company to develop a CSR strategy from scratch.

However, when I asked the question "What are your core competencies?" they weren't so sure. "We connect buyers to sellers," was an obvious choice, but it didn't really hit the nail on the head. We worked for a long time until they finally realized, "You know what we do? We create markets." Once we figured out that what they did was to create markets, the ideas just started flowing. Soon someone asked, "What markets could we create that could make for a better world?" The answer? Handcrafted products that paid a fair wage to the developing-world artisans. So eBay partnered with a company called World of Good. Through this partnership eBay was able to produce environmental or social return while earning a financial return for the company and developing a whole new customer segment—those who care about paying fair wages to artisans in their communities. It also gave the eBay brand cachet and coolness.

Whirlpool

Whirlpool's core business objective is selling home appliances, and a core competency is outfitting homes with appliances. It's very simple, and there's no reason to make this more complex than it is. Whirlpool has several partnerships, but its signature one is Habitat for Humanity. This partnership makes perfect sense. The more homes that are built, the more people are going to be buying home appliances. And the more people who buy appliances, the more money Whirlpool makes.

Whirlpool supports Habitat for Humanity with financial contributions, with in-kind donations of product, and through the Whirlpool employee volunteerism program, which is targeted to Habitat. When Whirlpool sends its employees out to volunteer in the community—which is fantastic viral branding for them—it sends them out on Habitat for Humanity builds. Whirlpool also donates an Energy Star washer or dryer to every Habitat-Whirlpool-built house. Not only is Whirlpool getting more appliances into the hands of consumers, it is getting *energy-efficient* appliances into the hands of consumers, appliances that will save them money on their power bills and have a positive impact on the environment.

The program is a win-win proposition for all involved. And Whirlpool didn't commit to this partnership for just a year or two; the company made a ten-year commitment. Here's something to keep in mind for chapter 11 on measuring: it's a lot easier to measure and show results for a ten-year commitment than for a one-time commitment.

Barclays

Barclays Global Investors was new to the United States, and its goal was to create a local community footprint as quickly as possible. When I asked the senior leaders my standard question, "What are your objectives?" their answers were clear: "We want to attract talent. We have a lot of really smart, really successful people, and we want to engage them on something that isn't just about money. We want to lay a strong local community footprint." Barclays is always on the lookout for young talent, and it wants to keep the high achievers it has.

When I asked the senior leaders to list Barclays' core competencies, they had an answer. They said, "It's easy for us to tell you because it is part of our mission. Our mission is to bring financial freedom to the masses." Once you know what Barclays' business objectives are, and you know what its core competency is, we could get creative. We thought about financial freedom. Immediately we thought about parts of society that don't have access to a way to achieve financial freedom. So if one of your challenges was, for example, to attract female employees into the heavily male-dominated financial services sector, you could spend less money on diversity programs by adopting a CSR strategy of bringing financial literacy and freedom to women and young girls. This is a strategy that might make sense for Barclays.

Nike

Nike has a phenomenal brand. The attributes that come to mind are things like athletic, fierce, edgy, muscular, strong, and fast. The words and images used in Nike's marketing communications match these brand attributes—images of strong, sweaty, muscular humans with edgy, challenging tag lines. The company's marketing and advertising groups work together in brilliant tandem.

When Nike was first hit with concerns in the media about human rights and sweatshop issues, it went out and did considerable work in the area of its supply chain and developing compliance and standards and codes of conduct. Then the company started to talk publicly about it. However, at Nike, the corporate social responsibility group originally operated separately from the marketing and advertising groups, with no integration or joint development of messaging. As a result, the company's CSR messaging was initially full of human interest, with happy, smiling people. For Nike, this is a significant disconnect, as it does not match the company's overall strategically developed and fiercely promulgated core brand attributes. It just doesn't fit its authentic brand.

Being authentic means knowing who you are and what your attributes are and knowing what your mission is. Then your CSR branding and communication and strategy should match that. If Nike's brand is about being edgy, then its CSR strategy should be equally edgy. But companies tend to develop a whole new brand or subbrand with their CSR campaigns, and they are not seen as authentic by consumers. CSR campaigns have to fit in with the branding the companies already have.

Summary

CSR is not yet a leading attribute in attracting stakeholders to a brand. It may never be a leading branding attribute. But CSR can still be a differentiating brand attribute. In the best of possible worlds, CSR can be linked to higher quality (higher-quality embroidery on your jeans produced by factory workers who are treated well and given proper lighting), lower price (energy-efficient appliances), and greater convenience (CFL light bulbs that have to be changed only once every ten years). When integrated with these traditional attributes, CSR can be a powerful differentiator, particularly in highly commoditized market segments.

Branding your CSR efforts should not be treated separately from your brands themselves. Think of your CSR branding as an extension of your core brand. CSR can also serve as a subbrand, which can be extremely difficult for your competitors to mimic, can justify higher margins, and can serve as your ultimate differentiator in the marketplace and raise you up above the noise.

But before you can move forward, you first need to know your company. Dig deep. Get to the core of what your company is all about. There you'll find your truths—and the foundation of your CSR efforts.

4

GET A GOOD FIT

> All citizens should have the opportunity to be active, but all will
> not respond. Those who do respond carry the burden of our free
> society. I call them the Responsibles. The Responsibles exist in
> every segment of the community—the ethnic groups, the unions,
> neighbourhood leaders, the businesses . . . but they rarely form
> a network of responsibility for the community because often they
> don't know one another across segments. They must find each other,
> learn to communicate and find common ground. Then they can
> function as the keepers of the long-term agenda.
>
> —John W. Gardner

Pedigree is a pet food company that has found a good fit for its CSR program. When you visit the Pedigree dog food Web site,[22] the first thing you'll notice is a large photograph of a dog, Echo, wistfully staring at you from behind a chain-link fence. Accompanying the photograph is the caption "Echo waited patiently for a loving family." You see, Echo has been abandoned and rendered homeless and now lives in a dog pound. It's easy to imagine that this rejected animal—probably a former family pet—is just days, or maybe even hours, away from a date with the gas chamber. Fortunately, the photo soon changes to a new one, in which Echo is playing outdoors in the grass on a sunny day. The caption for this photo reflects a happy ending: "It was worth the wait."

Another heart-tugging commercial, shown at times on TV and on the company's Web site, shows a big brown doe-eyed dog staring directly into the camera with an expression that says that he knows he is a good dog.

What he does not know is how he ended up in here—as the camera pans out to a four-by-four-foot chain-link cage in a dog shelter. When I show this commercial as part of my CSR and branding lectures, it has made even unemotional men tear up, its impact is so strong.

If you're a dog lover—and you probably are if you have visited the website and viewed the commercials—it will touch your heart. Looking through the site, which boldly promotes Pedigree's Adoption Drive—a partnership with the American Humane Association to encourage the adoption of dogs in animal shelters—you intuitively know that Pedigree is one of the good guys. And perhaps as a result Pedigree will earn your business.

Pedigree's main CSR strategy is centered around pet adoption, and its branding for this strategy is beautifully simple: help us help dogs. For this division of candy-making giant Mars, Inc., the strategy is a classic fit. It is clearly in Pedigree's interest to get as many dogs as possible out of shelters and into Pedigree dog food–buying homes. And it's in Pedigree's interest to be seen by consumers as a dog lover—one of the good guys, as are the consumers. If you visit the Pedigree Web site, you'll see that the company didn't just pick a cause and slap a label on a can of its Butcher's Selects Herb Roasted Chicken doggy dinner. There's substance behind the pet adoption campaign. On the Web site you'll find various educational tools focused on the topic of pet adoption. You can enter your zip code and find adoption shelters near you. You can see what kinds of dogs are best if you have young kids or no kids or elderly people in your house, or if you live in a tiny apartment or on a big farm.

When Pedigree looked for a cause to support, management first looked for an issue for which the company could contribute part of the solution, and something that would fit it closely—a cause with which its customers would naturally resonate. Once they decided on pet adoption, they looked for an established expert in the field, one that would bring issue and domain expertise and hence advance the company's capabilities and credibility. Partnering with the American Humane Association accomplished both of these goals. It's brilliant branding on Pedigree's part, and the campaign has substance behind it. But is Pedigree just trying to sell more dog food? Yes, that's certainly part of it, and that's good, because the program ties to the company's business success and won't get cut at a new CEO's whim or when the company experiences a down quarter. The program contributes to good business for Pedigree.

Furthermore, this Pedigree strategy elicits easy-to-do, immediate action on the part of consumers, and consumers love that. Even if I'm not in the market right now to adopt a pet, I know that I can go out and buy a bag of Pedigree dog food for the pet that I already have and that a percentage of that purchase will go toward supporting pet adoption. It's fast, it's easy, and it makes me feel good. All I have to do is buy a bag of dog food, and I've done it—I've helped save the life of an abandoned dog. What dog lover wouldn't want to make a difference in the life of an abandoned pet?

Narrowing the Brand Image Identity Gap

Do you know what your company's brand image is? Is it innovation? Speed? Strength? Low cost but high quality? Convenience? You probably think you understand your company's brand image pretty well. Now, what if you asked a group of, say, a thousand people chosen at random what their image of your brand is. What answer do you think they would give you? Chances are that your own idea of your company's brand image would not always be consistent with the ideas of others. The difference between what you perceive as your brand image and what others perceive it to be is called the *brand image identity gap*.

Jennifer Aaker, a branding guru colleague of mine, did some work with Google in this area. She asked a group of Google employees what they thought Google's brand identity was. Here are some of the responses from this group of Google insiders:

- Authentic
- Innovative
- Trustworthy
- Humble
- Responsible
- Quirky

It's all good, right? Well, it may not be. Aaker then asked a group of one hundred students in a research experiment what their brand image of Google was. While some of the responses were consistent with Google's self-image, others were decidedly different:[23]

• Search	• Arrogant
• Profitable	• Internet
• Innovative	• Creative
• Big	• Fun
• Powerful	• Cool
• Useful	• Ads
• Fast	• Free food

In Google's case—and certainly in the case of most large companies—some significant brand image gaps are revealed: humble and arrogant, responsible and cool, innovative and free food. Corporate social responsibility can help companies close this gap, bringing together the brand and attributes your company presents to the world with how the world perceives it. Perhaps Google could show its responsibility more effectively if it highlighted its Googleplex solar installation—the largest corporate solar installation in the United States—over its free-range eggs in the cafeteria. CSR can only be as effective as is the fit between your company and the cause and nonprofit partners you select.

Building a Foundation of Trust

The foundation of all successful businesses is trust. In its simplest form, trust comes from nothing more than delivering on a promise. The promise could be made to your employee, to your business partner, to your vendor, to your shareholders, or to your customer. Trust is the foundation of all successful business, but the public's trust in business to operate in society's best interest is at an all-time low. If you're running a business, this gap can be detrimental to your chances for success.

Trust is lacking for business right now. There's a general perception that business is not doing things ethically, not doing things with integrity, not doing things in society's best interest. Although it is not a panacea for this erosion of trust, CSR can play a significant role in filling this critical gap.

Your employees need to be able to trust that your company is the best place for them to work and that they will be valued and treated fairly. Your company's customers need to be able to trust that the promises made by your brand for its products and services will be kept. Your company's suppliers, retailers, and partners need to be able to trust that their dealings with you will be honest, fair, and of mutual value. Local and global communities and governments need to be able to trust that your company will be a good citizen. Future business leaders need to be able to trust in your company as a beacon of business innovation and savvy.

An authentic, well-executed CSR strategy can be indelibly linked to increasing and securing trust with all of your stakeholders. But if this well-developed CSR strategy is not communicated constantly, consistently, and to all, it cannot be effective in building trust or security. And if this CSR strategy does not fit with your business objectives, competencies, and brand image, it will not instill trust.

CSR can be an effective vehicle for establishing and maintaining trust and building credibility. Companies are going to have missteps from time to time, no matter how well they are run. By building trust through their CSR efforts—and banking the resulting goodwill—companies can weather the storms resulting from their occasional lapses. Hewlett-Packard has done a good job of building trust with its stakeholders. When the company went through a scandal in 2006 as a result of the alleged pretexting of the personal phone records of certain board members, this painful situation blew over relatively quickly, and with minimal negative impact to the firm. This result was at least in part because Hewlett-Packard had reputational credit in the bank.

I was working at HP during the summer when the scandal was unfolding, helping an executive team to refine HP's CSR strategy. The situation was demoralizing for workers who had to come to work when their company was on the front page every day for alleged ethical breaches. This feeling was balanced, however, by the fact that employees knew that HP was doing good things and making the world a better place, by supporting education and bringing technology to underserved markets. In fact, HP employee satisfaction surveys showed that doing things "the HP way"—that is, contributing positively to communities—was responsible for the high levels of job satisfaction. Employees felt that the work the company was doing was making the world a better place and that there was a firm commitment at the top to being a good corporate citizen. Attitudes like these can help companies buffer economic downturns, scandals, changes of leadership, and related events that tend to diminish employee morale.

In the end HP did have enough goodwill in the bank to avoid harm. In fact, it was not harmed at all. The share price sustained only minimal if any adverse impact. Of course, it went wild the day the scandal was announced, amid speculation about what was going to happen. But once the story unfolded, it quickly returned to normal. The same thing happened when John Mackey, CEO and cofounder of Whole Foods, was outed for using an alias while blogging against Wild Oats in the process of his company's attempt to acquire the company. This exposé and the resulting media attention ultimately had no impact on share price, and the government green-lighted the acquisition. Why was there little public outcry? Because Whole Foods had banked years of goodwill by being a good corporate and community citizen, and John Mackey himself had been a role model to other corporate leaders in showing that a company can simultaneously do well and do good. Whole Foods has been effective at communicating its message, so the trust and goodwill could be banked for future withdrawals.

However, when Nike found itself embroiled in scandal over its alleged use of sweatshops, its share price and brand suffered. Why? Because Nike didn't have a lot of reputational credit in the bank on which to draw. The trust just wasn't there.

Working Well with Others

One of my favorite, often high-impact CSR strategies is brand collaboration. You can be really innovative, reach across corporate lines, and partner with others in tackling highly intractable social or environmental problems (many of which are ultimately bad for business) like AIDS in Africa or the scarcity of clean drinking water in many parts of the world. Companies by nature don't work well with one another. They are by nature and training ruthlessly competitive in the marketplace. But we are seeing an increasing number of collaborative arrangements such as Product Red that are bringing companies together to solve problems on a global scale, problems that no one company can fully own or solve.

More than a decade ago, the U.S. apparel industry was hit hard with allegations of abuses in its global supply chain. Instead of banding together to solve the problem, each company independently went into self-protection mode, worked out a solution, and then rolled out the solution to much fanfare. For example, Levi Strauss & Company developed a code of conduct in 1991, becoming the first multinational company to establish comprehensive global sourcing and operating guidelines.

This achievement was certainly laudable, but think for a moment about what happens when other manufacturers do the same thing, creating their own codes of conduct. If you're running a clothing factory in China and your company is a source for a handful of companies—Gap, Nike, Levi Strauss, Lands' End, L.L. Bean, and Hugo Boss—all of a sudden you've got six different codes of conduct nailed to your factory wall. Which one do you follow, and when do you follow it? That's assuming that you can translate the codes of conduct, because all six are printed in English, and all your factory workers speak and read only Chinese.

The initial response of the apparel industry is an all-too-common one. Companies have historically operated this way—individualistically and independent of one another. They may be able to work well with one another, but only when it is in their interest to do so.

Then came the electronics industry, which actually learned what not to do from the apparel industry. Instead of waiting to be called out for abuses in its supply chain, the companies started working on potential problems before they blossomed into a public relations disaster. Not only that, but they considered the approach the apparel industry took, and they recognized that it was inefficient, resulting in lost economies of scale and unnecessary burdens (which can turn into unnecessary costs) on overseas factories. So the companies developed an industry collaborative called the Electronics Industry Code of Conduct: one code of conduct that the major industry players—Hewlett-Packard, Dell, Sun Microsystems, and others—signed on to. It was a smarter and an ultimately more effective way of doing things. Industry collaborations, while not easy, are powerful and efficient ways of helping both the companies and the societal issues that they are setting out to tackle.

Building Strong Partnerships

When Whirlpool partnered with Habitat for Humanity, it made a ten-year commitment to the relationship. My advice to business leaders who are partnering with nonprofits is to formalize these relationships by way of written agreements. These agreements should be transparent and formal partnership contracts, with a termination clause that gives the parties an escape clause for specific reasons contained in the agreement. In the case of Whirlpool and Habitat, for example, I imagine that there's a clause that allows Whirlpool to terminate the agreement if Habitat doesn't build houses at some predetermined level and is therefore not providing the anticipated impact. I imagine that Habitat, too, might be able to terminate the partnership if Whirlpool does not stay true to its promises. For example, Habitat might want a commitment for how many volunteers it could expect to get from Whirlpool and which kinds of appliances (I hope EnergyStar) and how many Whirlpool would donate to the organization. Evaluative metrics built into the agreement can help build a strong partnership—and sustain it over time.

Once companies understand their own goals, business objectives, and competencies and then determine a social or environmental issue for which they own part of the solution—for which there is fit—the next step is to find a credible partner or set of partners (nonprofit or other private sector players or both) who fit with the overall goals and solutions. Fit is still of utmost importance.

Consider B2B Too

Consumers instantly understand the connection between Whirlpool and Habitat for Humanity, or between Pedigree and the American Humane Society. However, they might not understand the connection between Dow Chemical and clean water. Why not? Because Dow Chemical is mostly a B2B (business-to-business) company that sells the majority of its products to other companies. I cannot walk into a store and ask for a product made by Dow Chemical. That Dow Chemical's customers are other businesses, however, doesn't make the company's contributions any less valuable. Indeed, they are big positives for their business customers who are also trying to upgrade their own CSR efforts. In B2B, as in other business, trust is still a valuable business driver.

Hewlett-Packard, for example, might source some of its plastics, such as casings for its printers or laptop computers, from Dow Chemical. HP has made a deep commitment to corporate social responsibility, so it makes sense that it would look for suppliers that have deep commitments to CSR and that it would factor this in when developing supplier contracts. HP knows the harm that plastics do to the environment, so it understands Dow Chemical's commitment to sustainability and its experimenting with biodegradable plastics, and it gets to share the spotlight a bit by sourcing Dow Chemical as a supplier. If you're a manufacturer who is selling to other manufacturers, this is an important consideration to keep in mind. Your buyers want to feel good too, and they may even have corporate guidelines that compel them to seek out vendors that provide quality products at a reasonable price *and* that have a commitment to CSR. Today it's not always about who can provide the least expensive products. Ultimately, business relationships are linked to trust, and while trust is critical for everyday consumer relationships, it's even more critical for enterprise relationships, the B2B side of commerce.

Choose the Right Partner

How do you pick the right partner? Just as businesses are ranked and rated in terms of who is best in their industry, so too are nonprofits. Some choices are easy and are unlikely to generate controversy. For example, when Mars, Inc., decided to create its Pedigree Adoption Drive, it had an obvious choice to put together a partnership between its Pedigree brand of dog food and the American Humane Association.

There are a number of online resources that can help in assessing the quality and capabilities of nonprofits. See the sidebar "Assessing Potential Nonprofit Partners" for some of the best.

However, before you look outside for partners, first see whom you already know and with whom you have relationships. You may find that you're already working with one or more organizations that are ideal for what you are trying to do. At least 90 percent of developing a good partnership with a nonprofit is having a good, trusting relationship. If you've already spent time, money, and effort on developing a relationship with one key nonprofit, drop the other partners and work more closely with that one. You are likely to increase your impact on the issue and on your business, not to mention making your task of developing effective metrics easier.

Nonprofits have a lot to offer their for-profit partners. They are expert in some social or environmental issue, and businesses generally are not. And when you look at the surveys on trusted institutions in society, nonprofits come out on top every time. People tend to believe what a nonprofit says and trust that its motives are good. People tend to distrust what a business says, even if it is the same thing, and assume that the company is trying to hide some bad deeds. The beauty of branding your CSR with a nonprofit partner is that your nonprofit can and should do much of the communication and branding for you, and the nonprofit will be believed. When exploring a partnership, you want both the company and the nonprofit to come to the table and bring with them the top five needs that they won't sacrifice. It pays to get each party's requirements on the table from the outset and to be transparent about them. The nonprofit should not be surprised if one of the needs on the list for its prospective business partner is to sell more product. Helping your partner achieve its goals will in turn help you achieve your own. However, the needs should be limited in number. A list of twenty or fifty or a hundred needs is going to be unwieldy. Keep the list to five at most, and be prepared to stick with them. Once you've each whittled your list down to the five needs you won't sacrifice, it's going to be a win-win situation for everybody.

Dove

When Dove looked for a partner for its Campaign for Real Beauty, it realized that it was not an expert on self-esteem. In fact, the people at Dove realized that they, along with the rest of the beauty products industry,

Finding the right nonprofit partner has fortunately become easier than ever when you take advantage of the many information resources available online. Here is a listing of some of the best.

- **GuideStar** (www.guidestar.org). The GuideStar database currently has information on more than 1.7 million nonprofits and can provide important information about the nonprofit's mission, programs, and finances. Of particular interest is the ability to view the most recent Internal Revenue Service Form 990 for many nonprofits. This form reports the organization's annual revenues, expenses, net assets, income-producing activities, program service accomplishments, and related information.

- **Charity Navigator** (www.charitynavigator.org). Charity Navigator provides ratings, using a system of zero to four stars, on more than five thousand nonprofit organizations. If the nonprofit earned four stars, then according to Charity Navigator, the organization is "Exceptional—Exceeds industry standards and outperforms charities in its cause." At the other end of the spectrum, a zero-star organization is "Exceptionally Poor—Performs far below industry standards and below nearly all charities in its cause."

- **Net Impact** (www.netimpact.org). Although not a directory of nonprofits like GuideStar and Charity Navigator, Net Impact is an international organization with the mission of making a positive impact on society by growing and strengthening a community of new leaders who use business to improve the world. Members include current and emerging leaders in CSR, social entrepreneurship, and related areas—a great group of people to network with.

had at least in some small part contributed to negative self-esteem in women. Whatever partner they selected would not only have to be expert in women's self-esteem issues but would also have to be a good overall fit with the company's values.

In the United States, Dove found the perfect partner: the Girl Scouts of the USA. For several years, the Dove Self-Esteem Fund has worked through the Unilever United States Foundation to sponsor *uniquely ME!*, a joint program with the Girl Scouts of the USA with the goal of building self-confidence in girls ages eight to fourteen. This program makes available a variety of self-esteem-building resources and program activities, including an online mother-daughter kit, which is a series of exercises that parents and children can work on together. This is an example of a brand campaign that has a partnership with a nonprofit expert in the actual issue. It has educational materials, it's got years of research behind it, and it's well-branded.

Product Red

Product Red started small, with just four partners: Gap, which had already been doing some work with the Global Relief Fund; Emporio Armani; Converse; and American Express. The organizers approached a number of big-name companies and got far more noes than they got yeses. For some companies, the idea of Product Red just didn't fit, with their image or with their product offerings. Other companies simply didn't want to be associated with AIDS or with Africa, or they didn't want to attach their brand to other companies' brands over which they had no control. Brand is a hotly protected asset for companies.

The night before the program was set to launch on *The Oprah Winfrey Show*, on October 13, 2006, Apple decided to join, despite the fact that the company had previously said no several times. It was a smart move. In the hour after the Product Red Oprah launch, e-commerce traffic on the Product Red company Web sites went up by 2,600 percent. What originally started as a collaboration of five brands has since expanded to nine, including American Express, Converse, Gap, Emporio Armani, Motorola, Apple, Hallmark Cards, Dell, and Microsoft.

As discussed in the introduction, Product Red is focused on AIDS and disease in Africa. Gap can and does contribute to the solution with its Lesotho factory project. Gap sources a significant number of its Product Red products from its Lesotho factories, thereby contributing to the economic development of that poor country. And when Gap goes into Lesotho and works with the government to set up apparel factories, the jobs it creates foster economic development, which brings with it schools and health clinics. Hence, it has an impact on AIDS and disease in Lesotho. That is the impact that one company, Gap, can have on its chosen social issue. Now imagine this impact multiplied several times with the involvement of eight other companies, and you can see the power of company collaboration.

Of course despite their good intentions, Product Red and the companies involved have not been without their critics. Some have said that the $50 million Product Red has sent to the Global Relief Fund is not enough. My view is that no matter what amount Product Red contributes to the Global Relief Fund, it would not be considered enough given the scale of AIDS and disease in Africa. However, the effort is not just about the money. We often forget that there are other measures of success besides money.

I like the Product Red model because it's about more than the money that's going to fight AIDS in Africa. It's about a new business model in which companies reach out to one another in the marketplace rather than doing what they're used to—trying to beat one another. It is a systemic, not an incremental, approach to solving world problems. With Product Red, these same companies are instead fiercely competing to work together to solve the social issues. When you consider the potential power that can be unleashed through companies collaborating, the impact can be world changing.

Dow Chemical and Coca-Cola

One of the main CSR issues that Dow Chemical is focusing on is clean drinking water. The company is trying to help the one out of five people in the world who suffer from a lack of this basic human need. Dow Chemical provides water filtration and purification systems—manufactured using its plastics—that are used to provide sustainable sources of clean water to communities around the world. This choice may have been in part a response to groups that have criticized the company for contributing to water pollution, but it is also a good fit for Dow Chemical's core competencies, which include plastics manufacturing and a worldwide distribution network. The company directly provides a solution for turning dirty water into clean water.

Consider Coca-Cola, which has also chosen water as its issue. Coke chose this issue largely because it has been singled out by the NGO community for having a water-intensive production process, thereby contributing to the problem, and the company produces bottled water products.

Imagine what would happen if you could get Dow Chemical and Coca-Cola to partner on clean drinking water—to start a collaborative along the lines of Product Red; call it Product Blue. In fact, that is what has happened. Taking the lead from projects such as Product Red, Dow Chemical and Coke have shrewdly started to collaborate and have found a nonprofit partner to partner with to advance their clean-drinking-water agenda: Blue Planet Run.

Blue Planet Run Foundation is a nonprofit 501(c)(3) organization dedicated to raising global awareness about the lack of safe drinking water and to funding working solutions for the one billion people living without ready access to this life-sustaining resource. Since 2004 this U.S.-based foundation has funded eleven nongovernmental organizations worldwide, and those organizations have in turn implemented 135 sustainable water projects in thirteen countries, impacting 100,000 lives. The foundation's signature awareness-raising and fund-raising event is the Blue Planet Run, the first-ever around-the-world relay run.

Starbucks would be a natural partner in this collaborative, as it has also undertaken a CSR initiative to provide safe water, having acquired the Ethos brand of bottled water in April 2005. Ethos Water was launched by social entrepreneurs Peter Thum and Jonathan Greenblatt (two friends whom I greatly admire), who had a social mission from the outset of helping kids get access to clean drinking water. Thum and Greenblatt sold Ethos to Starbucks in 2005 to help expand its reach, both in increasing sales and in providing access to clean drinking water for children. Starbucks joining the Blue Planet Run collaborative would be a great fit, but getting companies to collaborate and not compete (Coke competes with Ethos in the bottled water market) is a daunting task.

Summary

The world will never suffer from a lack of intractable challenges, problems, or opportunities. Your company, which—along with its fellow businesses—collectively controls the majority of the resources, will never suffer a lack of worthy causes. Indeed, the number of possible noble causes that need your company's support will always far outstrip its resources and abilities. It is for this reason and others that doing the preparatory work to determine fit is critical.

Know what your company does and does well. Know what its key core competencies are. Prioritize its business objectives. Then select a cause or opportunity for which it owns part of the solution, on which it can make a significant positive impact. Believe me, this will be a liberating exercise for you and your colleagues, for you will much better be able to say no—despite the urgency of the needs—to the myriad opportunities that come knocking by the day asking for money, product, and partnership.

By undertaking this exercise, you will be able to focus narrowly and deeply instead of broadly and shallowly. You will be able to develop a few key metrics and prove impact instead of having a smattering of metrics across the board that show little impact. And, most importantly, your messaging can be tight, simple, and consistent. The better the fit and the more consistent the messaging, the more authentic and credible the brand opportunity becomes.

5

BE CONSISTENT

Look to make your course regular, that men may know beforehand
what they may expect.

—Francis Bacon

Not too long ago, two companies came to the Haas School to recruit MBA students during the fall recruiting season, as hundreds of companies do in their quest for today's best MBA talent. The contrast in the companies' presentations highlights the importance of consistency in CSR messaging.

One of the companies was Dow Chemical, which brought a senior executive team comprising eight people, including the head of strategy, the head of brand, the head of finance, and other high-ranking company officers. At the company's presentation to our students, each one of these people got up and spoke about why Dow Chemical was a great place to work.

I didn't go to the presentation, but the next day I walked into the classroom before class started and saw that my students were abuzz about something. I asked what all the excitement was about, and they told me it was about the Dow Chemical presentation. One of the students elaborated: "Every single Dow employee who got up and talked said Dow has a three-pronged corporate strategy right now—'We're focusing on technology, innovation, and sustainability'—and about how that three-pronged strategy worked within the company and within that person's respective functional area, such as finance or brand."

Dow Chemical's corporate strategy is a particularly good one because it's an *integrated* strategy. It's not sustainability as a separate entity—it's sustainability as it relates to Dow Chemical's doing well as a company. The Dow Chemical leaders who got up to speak to our Haas MBAs talked about technology, innovation, and sustainability and how that impacts their jobs in finance, in brands, in strategy, and the students were amazed. Not only did they not expect this from Dow Chemical—the company forever tarred with Bhopal and Agent Orange—but the students had not previously heard this kind of consistent CSR messaging during the recruitment process.

Dow Chemical's message was simple and strategic, and that's why it had the key advantage of consistency. Companies often have strong CSR programs, but they never talk about them They talk about their brand, about their products and market, about their salary package—but their CSR values and mission are hidden on the back of their employee badges. The fact that the Dow Chemical representatives' message was consistent left my students in awe, particularly since Dow Chemical is such a large and old-line company. You might think that Dow Chemical would be using CSR more as window dressing to try to sweeten up a troublesome reality. However, the opposite is true. The company is serious about CSR—it's a big part of its organization and its corporate strategy.

Dow Chemical made offers to four of our MBA students, and four offers were accepted. That may not sound like a big deal, but Haas is a small school. Even our top recruiters take only nine of our students each summer. Not only that, try getting a San Francisco Bay Area–based twenty-seven-year-old to move to Midland, Michigan. Dow Chemical did!

The second company that came to Haas to recruit was McKinsey, the lauded consulting company for whom cream-of-the-crop MBA candidates vie to work. At the recruiting reception, the McKinsey representative gave his usual presentation about how great McKinsey is—highly regarded employer, challenging work assignments, work-life balance, and so forth. The third question from the MBA audience was about what McKinsey did in the area of CSR. The representative looked confused, for he was not aware of any customer service representative slots at McKinsey. The student helpfully added that CSR was "Haas-speak" for corporate social responsibility. To this, the partner nodded quickly, exclaiming that the company allowed its associates to go out and clean up a park in the community one Saturday morning each year. The MBA student, not satisfied, asked what the company might do the other 364½ days aside from this Saturday-morning park cleanup. The presenting partner, looking slightly annoyed, told the job candidates that they could give donations to their school alma mater—to Berkeley—and that McKinsey would match those gifts.

This typically quiet MBA student, who had clearly decided that she did not want a job at McKinsey, calmly asked again if there was anything else that McKinsey might be doing in the area of CSR. She asked these questions in front of an auditorium full of Millennials—a generation of people who care deeply about CSR. The McKinsey representative finally stated that he was not aware that the firm was doing anything else as part of its CSR effort. Palpable silence ensued in the auditorium, and a significant brand opportunity for McKinsey—branding to potential employees—was lost.

And the saddest part of this story? In fact, McKinsey does a great deal in the area of CSR. The partner was unaware of it, so this did not have to be a lost opportunity.

The Dove-Axe Brand Clash

Large multinational corporations often own a variety of different brands and sell products that have little or no relationship to one another. For example, Procter & Gamble sells everything from Iams pet food to Cheer laundry detergent to Gillette razors. Normally these brands don't bump up against one another in the marketplace. That is, it's unlikely that the claims of nutritional excellence made in a print ad for Iams kitty kibble will conflict with the claims made for a smooth shave in a television commercial for a Gillette Venus razor.

Sometimes, though, the claims do conflict.

As discussed in chapter 3, in 2004 Dove introduced its Campaign for Real Beauty. The campaign made quite a splash in the beauty products marketplace because it used ordinary-looking women—of all shapes, sizes, and ages—in its ads instead of the standard waif-thin, impossibly beautiful models that the industry had relied on to hawk its wares for decades. At the heart of the campaign was a desire on the part of Dove— and its parent Unilever—to build up the self-esteem of the young girls and women that the beauty industry had been undermining for so long. The message was loud and clear: You don't have to be a supermodel to be beautiful. Let's redefine the concept of beauty.

Dove's campaign garnered much attention in the media, generating countless newspaper and magazine articles, Web site and blog mentions, radio and television news features, and discussions and segments on shows such as *Good Morning America, The Early Show, Today, The Ellen DeGeneres Show, The View,* and *The Tyra Banks Show.* Oprah Winfrey even devoted an entire show to Dove's initiative. Much of this media attention was overwhelmingly positive and supportive of Dove's decision to use models that actually looked like the company's customers.

However, Dove's parent Unilever is a big company—with more than $51 billion in annual revenues, it ranks as number 120 on the Fortune Global 500 list—and another brand in its wide-ranging portfolio is Axe. This brand has a decidedly different marketing angle than does its corporate cousin, Dove—an angle that happens to be 180 degrees different from Dove's.

Axe is the world's most popular male grooming brand, and its roster includes such products as scented body spray, deodorant, and shower gel. Where Dove has chosen to use models who don't fit the norm for most advertisements for beauty products, Axe embraces the woman as a sex object, and the models it employs in its commercials and ads fit that mold. To get a feel for the Axe aesthetic, consider the answer to the question "What will Axe's improved fragrance do for me?" posted on the Axe Web site:[24] "Science shows that Axe's improved fragrance acts upon the female libido and stimulates the clothing-removal section of the female brain. Which means you can fulfill more of your manly desires. One application of the new improved Axe and you'll smell like a hunk of man candy all day long. Which is good, because babes like man candy. Lots."[25]

In fact, one of Axe's popular TV commercials, "The Axe Effect," showed hordes of beautiful, scantily clad women running through jungles, scaling mountainsides, and swimming oceans—all converging on a single man spraying a can of Axe product into the air while standing on the beach. Of the hundreds of models employed for this commercial shoot, I doubt that a single one of them could have come from Dove's Campaign for Real Beauty. Not one.

What message does the Axe brand image send to other Unilever brands, particularly Dove? What message does it send to employees throughout the Unilever organization and to the company's vendors, shareholders, and—perhaps most important—to consumers? What do people think when they realize that Dove and Axe are both Unilever brands and that the positive results Dove is creating with its self-esteem campaign are being directly negated by Axe, which is perpetuating the idealized image of women as rail-thin, big-breasted, flawless sex objects?

It's a good question. And it's one that has already been taken up on the ubiquitously viral site YouTube, on which an individual posted the two commercials—Axe's and Dove's—side by side, sparking hundreds of comments on the company's inconsistent messaging.

Consistency—the Best Policy?

Why should we care about consistency in a brand image? Does the image a brand projects really have to reflect reality, or the values of the company that employs it? Unilever owns both Dove and Axe. But while Dove is promoting the idea of redefining the ideal of beauty—reflecting the reality of what its customers really look like—Axe is selling an idealized version of sex, pure and simple. I have no intention of singling out Unilever here. I suspect the same inconsistency would hold true for every multiple-brand company. A company typically doesn't state that every product's brand message has to be the same. That would not be possible for products such as Proctor & Gamble's Iams and Gillette brands, for example. But brand messages certainly should not directly oppose and negate one another. That seems an inefficient use of expensive branding resources.

The challenge posed by the Dove and Axe brands is actually a perfect example of how a company isn't treating CSR as part of its overall business strategy. It points out the danger of inconsistency of messaging across brands. Unilever is still treating Dove's Campaign for Real Beauty as a separate case, not part of its overall business strategy for branding. One of Unilever's clear core competencies is branding. The company knows branding and does it extremely well. Dove has done a good job of not overplaying its campaign because to do so could lessen the impact of its message. Dove also runs its ads in different media, including print, billboards, television, the Internet, and more. In February 2006 it ran a commercial during Super Bowl XL—an expensive, high-visibility buy— that generated a nice buzz. Then the campaign went quiet for a while before doing more print advertising. It also created a viral film that got passed around on YouTube and the Internet with great success. Dove's messaging comes in various formats, but the message is consistent—the Dove Campaign for Real Beauty.

I believe that Dove and Axe will get to consistency one day. Unilever is a huge company that has made a significant commitment to CSR, with clear-cut goals and metrics. It has hundreds of brands in its portfolio. Am I suggesting that every product should be linked to redefining the perception of beauty? No. But the company's other brands shouldn't go *against* Dove's campaign to redefine the perception of beauty.

If a company builds CSR in its brand and communicates it, doesn't that mean it is hiding behind the good work it is doing while ignoring the bad? Not necessarily. No good deed goes unpunished. People ask me all the time, "Aren't you telling companies to just put up a smoke screen to hide despicable behaviors?" I say, no, that's not the case at all. With people's access to technology and information today, any company that thinks it could get away with that for longer than an hour before someone posts a YouTube video or creates a Web site pointing out the inconsistencies is naive at best and reckless at worst. The company risks tarnishing its brand when people figure out that it isn't exactly being forthcoming with them. The gap between your brand image and reality should always be kept to a minimum.

Consistency in What?

Consider Pedigree and the consistency of its pet adoption message. Pedigree is consistent in its message no matter who the recipient is, whether to consumers in its advertising, to prospective employees in its recruiting, or to food companies that are providing ingredients for its product. The message remains consistent when the CEO speaks at the annual sales meeting, to investors, to consumers, or to employees. And it remains consistent across brand channels, including point of sale, online, print, and television ads.

All the research suggests that creating a Web presence for CSR messaging is critical because that's where people are going first when they are researching a company's CSR messaging. Because companies have been so neglectful of communicating their CSR policies, people have had to seek this CSR company information out for themselves, and the Internet is where they go. This is not to say that if they get the message in a store they're going to ignore it, but the Internet is where they're going to go to corroborate what you're saying to see if you can back it up. Pedigree can have a blurb on a bag of Pedigree dog food and it can have a tear-jerking commercial, but the message really comes alive when you go online and see that the company has a pet adoption education guide and tons of resources available for people to get involved.

Most companies I work with have done a great job of developing their CSR messages on their Web sites and in their CSR reports. They are demonstrating a pull strategy for CSR communications, in which they are trying to pull and attract people to their Web sites. But even these companies have failed to consistently push their CSR communications and branding out to their stakeholders by way of in-store signage, point-of-sale messages, product hangtags, and so forth.

Debunking Myths at McDonald's

I once facilitated a dialogue at McDonald's in which I had all its key executive officers—including its CEO, president, chief human resources officer, chief marketing officer, and chief restaurant officer—around the same table. We were talking about all the CSR substance that McDonald's already has, particularly because of Ronald McDonald House Charities, which serves five thousand families with sick children each day, providing shelter, meals, and comfort to the families for extended periods of time for free. The charity operates in fifty-one countries and regions and has awarded hundreds of millions of dollars in grants and program services to causes that benefit children.

Despite the impact of Ronald McDonald House Charities, you can walk into a McDonald's restaurant in most any city and not see anything about those five thousand families served each day, or about the hundreds of millions of dollars spent on behalf of children all around the world. The turning point in our dialogue came as the CEO, James Skinner, was talking about the two most commonly held myths that he would most like to debunk about McDonald's.

The first of these myths was that the food served at McDonald's is, by nature, unhealthy. In fact, McDonald's has been the leading fast-food company in adding healthy product offerings to its menu—for example, salads, yogurt, and carrot sticks in kids' meals. Indeed, it was the first fast-food company to get rid of Styrofoam packaging, which is deemed bad for the environment, and all the other fast-food companies followed. It was the first fast-food company to get rid of supersized portions. Indeed, after McDonald's announced its decision, Burger King doubled its supersized product offerings and gained American market share. The CEO said that even the company's top customers—the people who give it the most business—get only 3 percent of their food intake from McDonald's. McDonald's is not responsible for the other 97 percent of these top customers' food intake. How could the company's branding be used more effectively to debunk the myths that food served at McDonald's is all unhealthy?

Another myth that he wanted to debunk was the concept of the McJob—the idea that McDonald's is a dead-end place to work. In reality, the company has a management training facility called Hamburger University in Oakbrook, Illinois. Hamburger University rivals even the top American colleges in terms of state-of-the-art facilities and campus amenities. Of the nine McDonald's executives gathered around the table, at least three or four of them started off as burger flippers, including company CEO James Skinner. So clearly working at McDonalds does not have to be a dead-end job for employees interested in partaking of the company's vast employee training and development offerings.

The McDonald's executives and I were chatting about this, and Mary

Dillon, the chief marketing officer, piped up and said, "You know what? That's brilliant. We have that commercial that shows a mentally challenged employee of ours and his successes on the job. It's a commercial showing that McDonald's reaches out to people with disabilities in its restaurants." She looked at the CEO and said, "We should run that as our Super Bowl commercial." The point was that the company was going to run a Super Bowl commercial anyway—and spend big money on it—so why not run a commercial that actually debunks some of the negative press about McDonald's? CSR doesn't have to be about new resources, new spending, new capital. McDonald's understands that it has the substance to talk about, and it can talk about it using already-committed resources that serve a two-fold purpose: to advertise and to build brand and reputation equity through their CSR.

But the McDonald's leaders were reticent to talk about that because they were afraid they would just be criticized. I countered, "Look, guys, you're McDonald's—the number one fast-food company in the world. You're going to get criticized anyway, so pick what you want to be criticized for. Actively recruiting and developing people with disabilities to get and maintain gainful employment is not such a bad thing for which to be criticized!"

An article in the *San Francisco Chronicle* in 2008 reported that the city wanted to pass a new law that would require fast-food restaurants to provide complete nutritional labeling for their products.[26] Supposedly this idea had fast-food chains (which, naturally, would want to continue to hide all the bad things they put in their food, right?) worried. The newspaper even used the McDonald's logo next to the headline of the story. In fact, McDonald's has been labeling its products since 2006, so it is way ahead of this progressive Bay Area legislation. It is not required by law to label its products. McDonald's did this on its own and went a step further. It came out with product labeling that was simple and easy to understand—far easier to understand even than the Food and Drug Administration's new version of the food pyramid. Clearly McDonald's has not been effective in communicating the story of its nutritional labeling.

So McDonald's has a great opportunity to build a consistent myth-debunking CSR messaging into its brand messaging.

Building Emotional Connection

When you are communicating consistently, stories trump facts ten times out of ten. We all like to show numbers and the logic of our CSR initiatives. For example, tea company Lipton is partnering with the Rainforest Alliance. What does that partnership look like? When companies communicate their message, they tend to talk about things like carbon sequestration or soil degradation, and consumer eyeballs begin to glaze over. Your message has no emotional impact when you present facts and numbers and esoteric concepts and processes.

Pedigree's CSR message is perfect because besides having substance, it is also simple and consistent and tugs at the heartstrings through the story of Echo the dog. It's a powerful brand blend. Everyone in branding knows that you want to have some sort of an emotional touchpoint, and CSR is no different. I think that because CSR is such a soft concept (yet we pretend it's not), ultimately we stay away from the emotional connection, and the message is just not as effective. We try to make CSR harder than it needs to be so it is viewed as being connected to the harder side of business—the financials. We go back to the numbers, to the facts, to the scientific data. We need to have the numbers on a Web site somewhere, but companies should not lead with them. It's great for Pedigree to have a picture of a sad dog sitting in a cage at an animal shelter, a picture that brings tears to your eyes and gets you emotionally involved. Then when consumers go to the Web site to check it out, they get all the facts about pet adoption and about the right dog for them, as well as see a real-time counter of the number of dogs adopted. You've got to have a blend of both soft and hard, but above all don't forget to make the emotional connection. And as they say in business, the soft stuff is always the hard stuff in the end.

Getting the CSR Message Out

Employees often make the best brand ambassadors. When Habitat for Humanity is doing one of its builds in a community, the Whirlpool employees who are out there helping build those houses for Habitat are brand ambassadors for Whirlpool. When a customer walks into a Starbucks and asks the barista, "What does fair trade mean?" or "What does Ethos Water do to provide kids with clean drinking water?" the employee becomes a brand ambassador when she knowledgably answers the question. Don't just use the company's communications as a brand ambassador. Use your employees and use your customers as consistent brand messengers.

One of the best companies at getting the CSR message out is Method Products. Method Products produces environmentally sound cleaning products that are sold at Target, Safeway, Costco, and other stores. Method Products is unique in that it has a formal brand ambassador program. Consumers can go online to the company's Web site[27] and become a brand ambassador. Being a brand ambassador simply means that the company will send the person samples of its products and a T-shirt. It wants people to use the samples and then go out and give samples to their friends and try to get them to use Method Products too. The company trains the person as a brand ambassador to tell others why the products are so much better than its competitors—because they aren't bringing toxic chemicals into people's homes and the chemicals aren't ending up in our rivers and oceans. Companies are learning now that getting your message out is more about relationship and lifestyle marketing and having your consumers speak for you and your employees speak for you. Having employees blogging about what they're doing on the job to make the world a better place is high-impact messaging that is much more credible than a traditional advertisement.

Companies themselves are not viewed as the most credible sources of CSR information. But if I walk into Starbucks and a barista can talk to me about what the company is doing in the area of providing access to water, then I just might believe what I'm being told. I know the founders of Ethos Water personally, so I was interested in how Starbucks would communicate its message after it acquired the company and started selling Ethos Water in its stores. Starbucks baristas are supposed to be knowledgeable about the company's products, so I decided to test their knowledge. I went into a local Starbucks, where there was a big barrel of Ethos Water right by the cash register. I bought a bottle and asked the barista to tell me about the Ethos mission of helping children get clean water—how exactly is that happening? His response? "I don't really know." This was a missed opportunity for Starbucks to get its CSR message out.

The effectiveness of that type of message is why Method Products got it right. The company has an army of brand ambassadors. If my girlfriend down the street is a brand ambassador of Method Products and she gives me some free samples and says, "Try this, it's really awesome, and it's not bad for the environment like all the other cleaning products in your cupboard," I'm likely to try it out. It's an inexpensive way for the company to get its CSR message out by a trusted channel—people's families and friends. How much do you think it costs to make me a brand ambassador and ship me a couple of boxes of samples every three months compared to what it costs to run a Super Bowl commercial? Here's a hint: it's a *lot* less expensive, and I'm more believable to boot.

My girlfriend works in branding at Dreyer's Grand Ice Cream, and we are always having conversations about what she can do to focus on corporate social responsibility (okay, maybe the conversations are more me giving her unsolicited ideas on what she can do). After all, Dreyer's produces ice cream, and she is the company's healthy snacks brand director. She called one day and said, "Do you know what I just found out? I found out that we've been using recycled cardboard for our ice cream boxes for a long time." And I said, "Well then, why don't you put that on your packaging?" You don't have to tell people that you're doing something that's socially responsible, but why not do it? It differentiates you from the competition. And when you do it, make sure it stands out and is visible— save the small print for the stuff that isn't important. Research tells us that consumers think recycling and recycled packaging are important. And, more importantly, Wal-Mart is telling its suppliers that they must both reduce their packaging and increase their recyclability to continue to be retailed at Wal-Mart. So it's a great time for Dreyer's to talk about its recycled packaging content.

Companies need to have a CSR messaging process that's integrated with their current advertising strategy and brand strategy that goes into print, media, online, and point of sale inside the stores. Although Whirlpool's campaign with Habitat for Humanity has for the most part been a good one, Whirlpool missed an opportunity in one critical aspect.

The campaign is a high-impact one—celebrity spokesperson Reba McEntire brought a lot of visibility to it. However, I talked to the people at Whirlpool, and they said there was a problem with the way consumers related to it. Consumers would walk into a Best Buy ready to buy a product and say, "I really like that Reba McEntire commercial about Habitat for Humanity and putting appliances into new houses, but was that a GE appliance, a Whirlpool, or what?" The problem was that there was no point-of-sale display keyed in to Whirlpool's campaign. When people arrived at a store to buy an appliance, they couldn't remember which brand to buy. As discussed, messaging needs to be consistent throughout all touchpoints, not just one or two.

The Buying Experience in Three Acts

The consumer buying experience has three distinct parts—prebuying, buying, and postbuying—and companies need to consider the consistency of their messaging across all of them. Companies tend to focus on the prebuying experience, which is what Whirlpool did in its commercial publicizing its relationship with Habitat for Humanity. Other companies, such as Fetzer Vineyards, concentrate on the buying experience. For its organically sourced wine called Bonterra, Fetzer developed a hangtag promotion in which it put a hangtag on the bottle of wine that pointed out the fact that the wine came from organically grown grapes. Fetzer didn't do any prebuying promotion because it doesn't do print or media advertising at all. And it doesn't do anything once the consumer buys the wine either.

Pedigree, on the other hand, hits all three parts of the consumer buying experience. A consumer can have a prebuying experience with Pedigree by watching a commercial. Or the person can have a buying experience by going to a pet store and seeing on the Pedigree product packaging that $1 of every bag purchased goes toward pet adoption. Or the person can have a postbuying experience by going to the Web site and looking at all the adoption guides and the adoption information that the company provides. Ideally, your advertising campaign should hit all three parts of the consumer buying experience, and your message should be consistent throughout the various touchpoints and customer experiences.

Keep in mind that good PR beats advertising, and it is far less expensive. Perhaps it's no surprise that the research shows that advertising is viewed as not necessarily believable or credible by everyone. The advertising might appeal to the emotions—as does the Pedigree commercial with its sad dog sitting in an animal shelter, hoping for a new family—but consumers often just think to themselves, "I don't know how deep this goes. This could just be a cheap way to get me to buy Pedigree dog food." But then they can go to the Pedigree Web site and see that the company's commitment runs much deeper.

This approach is a part of Pedigree's overall PR strategy, which is designed to generate consumer buzz and articles and mentions in the press and media. Pedigree has partnered with VolunteerMatch[28] to provide animal shelter volunteering opportunities to visitors to the Pedigree Web site, and it also has its own in-house employee volunteer programs—again run by VolunteerMatch—that are consistently focused on animal welfare. Pedigree's campaign has a high impact when its volunteer opportunities are all centered around pet adoption, because the media will pick up stories about Pedigree employees working to clean up an animal shelter or walking the dogs or standing on street corners with adoptable dogs. These stories are consistent with the fact that the brand stands for pet adoption, and they are much more credible in the eyes of consumers than any amount of advertising the company does.

Although some companies think that once they sell the product they're done, others do a particularly good job with the postpurchase experience as well. MINI Cooper drivers are a tight-knit community, almost cultish in their love for their cars. MINI partnered, again with VolunteerMatch, to host what it called a "ram and run," a campaign for MINI Cooper drivers where if you logged X number of hours of volunteer time through VolunteerMatch, MINI would send you a gold heart that you could affix to the back of your car. I think the idea was brilliant—a visible sign that you belong to a special group within this already special group of car buyers. It's a tie-in back to driving a MINI, and it's unique because while it's a community builder, only other MINI Cooper drivers who understand the meaning of the gold heart know that the person is in the club. One thing is for certain: the next car that the person buys—or the car the person recommends to a friend or neighbor—is going to be a MINI.

Levi Strauss & Company has always promoted employee volunteerism internally, and this has done wonders for employee satisfaction, engagement, and retention. Who wouldn't want to work for a company that is changing the world for the better? But for the first time that I've ever seen, Levi Strauss launched a campaign to get its customers involved in volunteering in their communities. Levi Strauss has named May 1 as 501 Day—a day designated by the company for employees from Levi Strauss & Company's headquarters, offices, and stores across the country to volunteer with community-based nonprofits. VolunteerMatch set up a Web-based platform where you can log on, enter your zip code, and find the various volunteer opportunities in your area where you can go out and work alongside Levi Strauss employees.[29]

This approach is particularly effective because Levi Strauss isn't just telling consumers what it does, and is not just showing consumers what it does, but is saying, "Do it *with* us." VolunteerMatch is the quintessential volunteer matching Web site, and it has set up many corporate platforms, providing the services behind many corporate volunteer sites. I think it's so effective in running corporate platforms because a potential volunteer can log on to VolunteerMatch.com anytime and find volunteer opportunities closely matched to her personal mission. She simply enters her zip code and enters her interests—for example, the environment, women, youth, or education—and specifies when she is available to work, whether weekends, evenings, or during the day. The system will immediately provide her with listings of opportunities based on what she input. And VolunteerMatch, as the back office for your employee volunteer programs, gets and activates branding.

Consumers today are looking for a relationship, not just a transaction. A CSR program can be an effective way to build relationships because it's hard to build a relationship only around the act of buying a pair of jeans. What are you going to say to your customers: "It's been a year; go buy another new pair of jeans"? Or would it be better to say something like "It's been a year; be sure to take time to volunteer on 501 Day and help your community"? And when you send your customers this message, you also link them to your Web site, where there happens to be news about those new flap-pocket jeans you just launched. It's important to always keep an eye toward business value as well as social value.

Educating Your Sales Force

Companies have two key opportunities to communicate their CSR during the consumer buying experience: through product packaging and through their sales forces. Working with the sales force—particularly a sales force that actually works for the retailer that sells your products to customers—can be challenging. Gap has struggled with this because it has a high number of seasonal workers and a high turnover in its retail outlets. But having a sales force who can talk authoritatively to customers about what Product Red is when you have a big Product Red display inside of a Gap store is critical. Education is an ongoing struggle for companies, especially in the retail industry, but when done right the impact can be high.

Companies often find it difficult to fully educate their entire sales forces, especially retail sales forces they have no direct control over such as the employees at Target, Wal-Mart, or Home Depot. However, a company like Pedigree *could* figure out its top two retailers—say it's Wal-Mart and PetSmart—and then do some focused education to the salespeople in these high-leverage locations. The way it typically works today is that companies send boxes of flyers and posters to retailers of their products, but they lose control over the educational process after that. Much of this educational material undoubtedly ends up unopened in some warehouse or in a dumpster in back of the store. You don't have to educate every salesperson, but you could accomplish a lot if you just picked the top two retail outlets.

You also get additional benefits by focusing your efforts on a high-impact player like Wal-Mart. Wal-Mart is trying to create a niche and become a socially responsible company. It is trying hard to create a name for itself in CSR. Putting serious effort into educating its salespeople would be a way for Pedigree to endear itself to Wal-Mart. Pedigree might also point out to Wal-Mart that its product promotes pet adoption and it might request premium shelf space over Company X, which doesn't have any sort of social responsibility program. The pet adoption program becomes a point of differentiation that adds to Pedigree's business value in the eyes of Wal-Mart. Wal-Mart has already shown an interest in doing something like this—it gave General Electric's energy-efficient compact fluorescent light bulb (CFL) premium positioning in its stores. The arrangement was profitable for GE, which sold more product, and it was advantageous for Wal-Mart, which was able to demonstrate that it takes corporate social responsibility seriously.

Summary

You are most likely already in the habit of managing your company's messaging, and hence its reputation, strategically and consistently, and are spending a great deal of money doing so. Think of CSR as another component of this strategic communication and messaging management. Perhaps it can even be one of its most important components. Companies always fear being perceived as self-serving, inauthentic, and not credible. Repetition has long been known to be one of the most effective tools of persuasion. Particularly with CSR communication and branding, consistency is key. Once you have engaged deeply with all stakeholder groups and have selected the well-fitting causes and opportunities, constantly and consistently communicating a simple strategic message will add value. This means integrating your CSR message with your core branding strategy to consumers, of course, but this also means communicating a clear, consistent message to employees, to potential employees, to suppliers, to retailers, to governments, to communities, and to peers.

Dow Chemical Company communicates a concise message of technology, innovation, and sustainability no matter who the audience is. To consumers, the message is embodied in the company's Human Element campaign. To its board of directors, the message is communicated in terms of integration with the company's growth strategy. To employees, it is communicated in terms of what they should be focused on and for what behaviors they will be recognized and rewarded. To suppliers, it is communicated in terms of trust and relationship. The same core message is communicated across all stakeholder groups, consistently and regularly.

6

SIMPLIFY

Everything should be made as simple as possible, but not simpler.
—Albert Einstein

Go into any Starbucks, order a $5 vente double decaf, no-fat, no-foam, no-whip vanilla latte, move down the counter to wait for your order, and you will probably find a copy of the Starbucks corporate responsibility brochure strategically located by the sugar, cinnamon, and chocolate sprinkles. This brochure is an example of the type of complex CSR messaging that most people will not bother to read.

Starbucks has always been one of the companies that take social responsibility seriously. Starbucks made a name for itself years ago by providing health care, paid vacations and sick leave, company stock options, a retirement plan, and other benefits to part-time workers—benefits unheard of in the quick-serve restaurant industry. And while most companies have one mission statement, Starbucks has two. The first is the standard kind you would find in almost any business, with an emphasis on providing a great work environment for employees and developing satisfied customers and so forth. The second is an *environmental* mission statement with an emphasis on CSR:

> Starbucks is committed to a role of environmental leadership in all facets of our business.
>
> We fulfill this mission by a commitment to:
>
> * Understanding of environmental issues and sharing information with our partners.

- Developing innovative and flexible solutions to bring about change.
- Striving to buy, sell, and use environmentally friendly products.
- Recognizing that fiscal responsibility is essential to our environmental future.
- Instilling environmental responsibility as a corporate value.
- Measuring and monitoring our progress for each project.
- Encouraging all partners to share in our mission.[30]

You might not be surprised to learn that Starbucks also publishes a corporate social responsibility annual report. The full 2006 edition runs seventy-seven pages and can be viewed on the Starbucks Web site.[31] If English isn't your first language, you can also download an abridged version of the CSR annual report in a number of different languages, including Spanish, Arabic, Chinese (simplified or traditional), and Japanese.

In this report Starbucks effectively makes a case for why corporate social responsibility is important and why the company pursues it aggressively:

- **Attracting and retaining our partners.** We believe Starbucks' commitment to CSR leads to higher than typical levels of satisfaction and engagement among our partners.
- **Customer loyalty.** Studies have revealed that customers prefer to do business with a company they believe to be socially responsible, when their other key buying criteria are met. We believe customer loyalty has been a driving force behind Starbucks' phenomenal growth and long-term success.
- **Reducing operating costs.** Many environmental measures, such as energy-efficient equipment or lighting, involve initial investments, but deliver long-term environmental and cost-saving benefits.
- **Strengthening our supply chain.** To have a sustainable business, we need a reliable and responsible supplier base that can keep pace with our growth. Starbucks invests in measures to ensure our suppliers have the opportunity to do so.
- **License to operate.** Having a strong reputation as a socially responsible company makes it more likely we will be welcomed into a local community.[32]

Starbucks' CSR annual report is a lengthy, detailed, and complex document—too long for most people, even busy professors of corporate responsibility. Chances are that few customers or even Starbucks employees will actually take the time to read it from cover to cover. Fortunately, the downloadable version can be read online, and no trees have to give their lives for you to have the privilege. Even the CSR in-store brochure is set in 10-point type, multifold, jam-packed with information and graphs, and not very pleasing to the eye. The brochure is not effective as branding or communication. It does have its purposes, as will be discussed, but one of them is not floating above the noise and reaching busy customers, or even employees.

Instead, why not communicate its CSR message using the simple one-line epithets that Starbucks is now placing on its recycled-paper cups? I guarantee you that far more—the majority, even—of Starbucks customers would read that coffee cup while sitting at their desks at work, while procrastinating, or while sitting at a Starbucks table waiting for colleagues. When you're trying to communicate your CSR message, simpler is better.

Where the CSR Movement Fails

Simplicity is where I think the CSR movement as a whole has failed, and where it should focus for maximum impact. In fact, I was on a plane recently and was reading a magazine. I came across a two-page spread that discussed the problem with honeybees, their disappearance, and the impact on one-third of the world's food supply that depends on them to pollinate fruit, vegetables, and flowers. I read only half of the probably costly two-page spread, which showed a container of Häagen-Dazs ice cream, and continued leafing through the magazine.

I turned the page and saw an eye-catching Skinny Cow ice cream advertisement, replete with a cute lipstick-wearing cow lying on its side and calling out to me to indulge: I deserve it, it's low fat, and it's nearly guilt free. This was an ad, it was clear, and it reached me (full disclosure: my friend, whom I mentioned earlier, is brand director for Skinny

Cow, so I had another reason for liking the ad, besides the fact that it is a great ad).

But the Häagen-Dazs brand is owned by Dreyer's. And that two-page spread announcing the problem with disappearing honeybees? It was actually an advertisement, not an article, despite its appearance. Even I, who am attracted to socially responsible articles and ads, did not read more than half of the expensive Dreyer's media spread. Why didn't Dreyer's engage its branding department—full of brilliant brand directors like my friend—which knows that in branding to rise above the noise and make an impact, two-page spreads filled predominantly with text and clip-art pictures of bees won't work? What *would* work is to integrate the company's commitment to this significant and timely world-food-supply issue into its advertising and brand.

Too many companies have made their CSR strategies, program, reports, and communications far more complex than they need to be. I believe that simple messaging is the best. First, simple messages are easy to transmit and communicate—both inside and outside the organization. Second, simple messages get read. Third, simple and concise messages have more impact on the reader than do complex text-heavy, table-heavy, and graphics-heavy messages.

Unfortunately for the current state of the corporate social responsibility movement, many companies produce CSR reports that are eighty or ninety pages or more, reports that nobody reads except for one employee of an activist group and one socially responsible investment research analyst. These reports serve as internal strategy-setting and current-assessment tools, they look great, and they are certainly weighty, but for the most part they miss the mark completely as effective branding or communication tools. I have led numerous executive roundtable sessions with company unit heads of big companies who haven't even read *their own company's* CSR report in its entirety. They admit to having read only the sections that they were responsible for, the sections that involved their own business units.

I am not denying the usefulness of a big CSR report. As I said, the report can be a fantastic exercise and organizing tool to help companies understand what they're currently doing in their communities; what they're currently not doing; and where they might have gaps, opportunities, and inconsistencies. But many companies have overcompensated, often in reaction to the prodding of an NGO that has a problem with something the company is doing. Many companies mistake CSR reports for CSR communications, storytelling, and branding. Rarely do the twain meet. For Nike the issue was sweatshops. For Starbucks it has been paying its coffee suppliers a fair price for their coffee beans. For Chevron it has been finding alternatives for petroleum fuel sources. But for none of them has their response been effectively linked to their core brand, which can be traced to upwards of 80 percent of their value.

In most cases CSR reporting is ineffective for the majority of the company stakeholders—employees, customers, shareholders, suppliers, and others. CSR reporting is an effective tool to speak to the NGO community and to answer its concerns. It's also an effective tool to speak to the socially responsible investment community that wants to thoroughly vet companies before they invest in them. It is a strong strategy-development tool. But the typical CSR report is unsuccessful as a vehicle to communicate to consumers or employees. Ninety-page reports are *not* simple; nor are they read in today's world.

CSR reporting and branding are two completely separate things, and company leaders need to keep that in mind. Some companies put together ten-page executive summaries of their ninety-page CSR reports, which is better, but still few people have the time to read even ten pages in this day and age. You do have as a model Starbucks, which publishes a brochure on the company's corporate social responsibility efforts and places it conveniently where customers wait to pick up their drinks after they're prepared. But even this approach is imperfect. Not only is it a ten-fold brochure set in small type, but it talks about things like labor standards and fair trade—things the average consumer just doesn't understand.

When GlobeScan, a public opinion research firm, conducts its annual global survey research in the arena of CSR, the majority of consumers anywhere in the world identify first with CSR meaning "fair treatment of workers." Fair-trade coffee could be more effectively branded by Starbucks as simply "fair worker treatment" to garner more consumer attention and better understanding.

Starbucks, even as a leader in CSR, has missed an opportunity. If Starbucks had simply stated the catchy little epithet on their cups that "The workers who produced this coffee you're about to drink were treated and paid fairly," that would have been the perfect combined brand and CSR message. That's what I mean by simple. A term like *fair trade* by itself fails to rise above the noise and grab consumers' attention. When you tell them clearly and simply on the vessel that holds their yummy non-fat latte, however, that the worker who picked the coffee beans in some remote Central American field was paid fairly, people can understand that. They understand because at the end of the day we all have been, are, or will be workers who want to be treated fairly. And while drinking their $5 cup of coffee, consumers feel better knowing that workers who grew the coffee beans were paid fairly and were able to put food on their family's table and send their kids to school. It really is that simple.

Making It Simple

The simple message of Pedigree's pet adoption program is the reason it works so well. The message is this: help us help dogs. It's easy to understand that buying this bag of dog food contributes to pet adoption and that contributing to pet adoption saves animals' lives. Not only is the message simple, but the action that consumers are requested to take is simple as well. All I have to do as a consumer is buy a bag of dog food—a product that I already need to buy anyway because I have a dog and she needs to eat. I don't need to research the best and the worst nonprofits in pet adoption, or write a check and mail it out, or go online and write a letter to my state senator. I just need to pick up the bag and put it in my shopping cart. Check. I feel better. Or I just need to work for this company as a brand manager, financial analyst, or sales rep.

Consumers and employees want and need simple messaging—consistent messaging—and simple actions that they can do to become a part of your process and attempt to make a profit, and change the world. Often CSR departments are completely separate or divorced from brand departments, marketing departments, and ad agency relationships. This separation presents a significant problem. When CSR managers are not working side by side with brand managers, you end up with a situation like the one at Nike, with the Nike brand being promoted as fierce, edgy, competitive, and muscular while the CSR communications department is putting out flowery feel-good messaging. Instead of sending the message about doing fierce and edgy CSR work, the message is instead about factory workers being given ample time for breaks. Or worse yet is the situation at Unilever, where the Dove Self-Esteem Fund, the fund-raising arm of the Campaign for Real Beauty, carries a message that is in direct opposition to that of Axe's message that deodorant equals immediate attraction of scantily clad women. These messages just don't fit.

Whereas companies view brand as part of their integral business strategy, and that business strategy is often managed with close attention to detail, they still aren't viewing CSR as part of their integrated business strategy. When a typical corporation sets up a CSR group or department, it usually brings people in from the outside—perhaps a few leaders from a local nonprofit. Or it designates an employee from another department to take responsibility for the company's CSR efforts, often on a part-time basis in addition to the person's full-time appointment. Such arrangements provide little competency or time for attention to detail. The CSR program is disconnected, happenstance, haphazard, reactive, and all over the map.

The companies that do the best job of developing their CSR strategies work with critics and NGOs that might be tracking them or monitoring them closely. In the best scenario, a company brings in an outsider—somebody who might understand the issues that the CSR effort is dealing with, such as a factory representative from China or farmer from Peru—as an adviser or engaged stakeholder to help develop the company's strategy. It also designates someone inside the company who understands deeply the company's business model, supply chain, and sourcing system. The company in this scenario blends the best of both worlds, combining the expertise of an insider who understands the company business model, objectives, inner workings, and culture with an outsider who is an expert on the issue with which the company has wisely chosen to deal.

The Not-So-Simple Oil Industry

One industry that has missed this concept of keeping it simple is the oil industry. Almost every consumer understands the environmental degradation and social (read: political and security unrest in dangerous parts of the world) impact of oil, but oil companies are coming out with CSR messages that are fuzzy at best and confusing at worst. Chevron first came out with a campaign that seemed all talk and little substance. It had a campaign that it called Human Energy, but it showed no examples of what Chevron had successfully done as part of the campaign. There was no message to convey. This is an example of how you can be too simple in your CSR messaging, which is what occurs when there is no substance or real message to convey.

Chevron ran a number of expensive full-page ads in newspapers such as the *Wall Street Journal* in which it talked about the energy crisis, how bad the crisis was, and how we're going to run out of oil if we continue at our current pace. But that was it—no prescriptions, no to-do lists for consumers, no reporting of what the company was doing to help solve this problem. People were left with a big question: what are you doing about it? They might have gone on to ask another question: isn't your scariest question as a company who profits on the finite supply of oil?

Eventually the company realized that it needed to do more. That's when it started talking about things like carbon sequestration and trading of carbon credits. Sadly, few average citizens, even *Wall Street Journal* readers, fully understand the worth of these concepts. And that's where the CSR movement, and companies trying to communicate their CSR substance and story, are missing the boat. CSR needs to be described in simple and plain terms.

For example, in 2008 Chevron signed a significant sponsorship with the Tiger Woods Foundation, which supports science and math education of at-risk youth. Chevron's leaders understand that it behooves them to educate a population of future Chevron employees who know about science, engineering, and technology. The foundation focuses on this need, rightly stating that there is a lack of effective science, technology, and engineering education being offered in our public school system.

The connection between the Tiger Woods Foundation and Chevron's Human Energy campaign makes sense: Tiger Woods is igniting human energy, and he is able to do it more effectively now with Chevron's (we hope) deep commitment. That is substance that brings branding to life and lends humanity to this member of the big, bad oil industry.

Scientist Peter Senge once gave one of the best and simplest stories to describe global warming. He said that putting CO_2 into the atmosphere is like putting water into a bathtub that's already been half-filled with water. What happens when you continue to pour more and more water into the bathtub? It eventually overflows. This is a perfect analogy for our atmosphere, which already has a lot of CO_2 in it. Just like the bathtub, if you keep putting more CO_2 into the atmosphere by heating monstrous houses, filling up Hummers and Ford Expeditions, and buying food shipped to Kansas from Africa, the bathtub that is our atmosphere will eventually overflow, causing who knows what kinds of catastrophic environmental damage. The idea is so simple that even my six- and eight-year-old daughters understand it.

Good for the Earth; Good for the Bottom Line

You've no doubt noticed the little signs in hotel bathrooms that ask you to do your part to save the environment by hanging up your towels after you use them. Hang your towels on the towel rack, and the maid will assume you would like to reuse them and will not replace them with newly laundered ones. Throw them on the floor, and the maid will replace them with clean ones. When you hang your towels up, you may be doing your part to save the Earth by reducing the demands on the resources that go into the washing of those towels, but you're also helping the hotel save money. A towel that sits on your towel rack instead of being washed and dried is a towel that enables the hotel to spend less on water, electricity, and the labor required to launder it. Dreyer's ice cream shop doesn't want us to use its napkins unless we really need to, as they cost the shop money and the environment trees.

While some people might see these types of CSR programs as a subversion of the precepts of corporate social responsibility, I strongly disagree.

When a CSR strategy saves the company money, the company is more apt to push it and to support it than it would be if the strategy costs the company money. To be truly sustainable a CSR program has to be profitable and to be truly socially responsible it has to contribute something good to society or to the environment.

Still, people often try to divorce CSR from the need to build a healthy business. Teaching a class one Monday night, I was shocked by my students' reaction after I showed the Dove ad, followed by a series of high-impact self-esteem ads showing eight-year-olds talking about how fat they felt and thirteen-year-olds talking about being told they were ugly by schoolmates and how that made them feel. The first comment was "I hear that Dove didn't really do this to increase self-esteem in women or work to change the distorted perception of beauty. It did this to sell more products, to differentiate itself from its competitors' brands, and it just got lucky. It hit upon a campaign that made it a lot of money."

I responded, "Why does it matter so much *why* Dove did it? If the campaign does differentiate it, that's awesome—that's why the company has *kept* doing it. If the missing metric in all this is whether or not the campaign is having a positive effect on self-esteem in young girls and women, that's a justified question that Dove, if it is wise, is measuring. We know it affected *you*. Each one of you in this room was wrapped up in the commercials I just played for you."

In fact, I have played these commercials a thousand times, and I am still affected every time I see them. I think back to last year, on the second month of kindergarten, when my five-year-old daughter came home complaining that her thighs were fat. She had never even used the word *thigh* before that day. I asked her why she thought that. She told me some older kids told her that on the playground. So as a mother of two girls, I absolutely know that we *need* to foster positive self-esteem around the image of beauty in women and young girls. If Dove is going to commit itself to this cause; to partner with the Girls Scouts; to dedicate time, staff, and resources to this, then it had better sell more product, engage and motivate more employees, and get more brand differentiation from it, because I want the company to continue to do this.

People get too caught up in motivations. My job is to try to get them to focus instead on outcomes. When I'm working with a specific company, I do want to know what its motivations are, but when I'm judging whether a company's CSR effort is strategic or not, I'm much more focused on whether or not there is a measurable impact, both on its chosen social or environmental issue and on the company itself. What are the outcomes? If there is a positive impact on the environment or society as well as a positive impact to the company, then to me it qualifies as strategic, smart, and sustainable.

Differentiating Your Company in the Marketplace

Think for a moment about General Electric and its launch of Ecomagination—the company's vision and commitment to harness its global capabilities, technology leadership, and market knowledge to take on some of the world's toughest problems, and to accelerate company growth while doing so. Why did GE choose to go green? Why did the company decide to make more-energy-efficient products?

The price of oil has reached all-time high peaks in price, and it looks as if it will continue to rise. The environment is being degraded. Greenhouse gases are on the rise, and global warming is now considered a fact in most quarters. Increasingly, the environment is becoming one of the main things that consumers are concerned about. GE knows that it can differentiate itself in the marketplace because its competitors aren't focusing on the environment. This differentiation gives the company an opportunity to significantly increase revenues and profits, thus making the business case for going green. And if GE generates some positive press and customer goodwill in the process, that's the icing on the cake and is the thing that will ultimately motivate GE to dedicate more resources to Ecomagination.

The rationale behind corporate social responsibility is going to be different for every company. It's up to you and your colleagues to put together the best business case for your company based on your unique drivers, needs, and objectives. This goes back to the principle discussed in chapter 3: know thyself. You need to figure out what your company's core business objectives and core competencies are, and then you need to show how CSR can provide a match. Understand that CSR is never going to be the universal panacea for all of your corporate needs, but by becoming a vital part of your company's business strategy, CSR can (and will) help satisfy your business objectives while leveraging your core competencies.

Sometimes the easiest and fastest way to justify a CSR program is also the simplest: your competitors are doing it. When I and others were trying to provide justification for CSR to Meg Whitman at eBay, I kept hearing from her employees "Meg only wants the data," "You've got to show her numbers," and "You need to show her what this is going to do in terms of numbers for our growth and market penetration." We showed her all that, but as it turned out, the presentation slide that turned the tide was the very last one in our ninety-slide deck. This slide showed what Yahoo! and Google were doing in the area of CSR and how very far behind eBay lagged. Suddenly Meg got it, and she became a supporter.

Pedigree has differentiated itself in a crowded market with its simple but compelling message of getting dogs out of shelters and into homes: "Help us help dogs." Buy a can or bag of Pedigree dog food, and you're going to help save the life of a dog. The message is so simple that even my six-year-old daughter gets it. She sees Pedigree's pet adoption commercial on TV, and a couple of things happen. First, she tells us to buy Pedigree. Second, she asks if we could go volunteer and walk dogs in a shelter. Third, she tells her friends about this Pedigree commercial and how they might want to help homeless doggies. And when she grows up and gets her own dog someday, I wouldn't be surprised if she feeds it only Pedigree products.

Recall the picture in the Dreyer's ice cream shop shown in Figure 7. A simple drawing, one of many made by local school children, has had a measurable and lasting impact on our family and our community. The drawing made sense to my daughter, who was old enough to understand that paper came from trees and that the more paper you use, the more trees get cut down. And the more trees that get cut down, the more animals lose their homes. I do not think that the Häagen-Dazs two-page text-laden spread about the disappearing honeybees has the same impact. Glossy ads and ninety-page CSR reports have their place, but when you're trying to reach the hearts and minds of your customers, simple is better.

REI

REI, the outdoor equipment retailer, has built its entire advertising campaign around protecting the environment. This cause is a good fit because the company's products are used by people who are enjoying the environment, the outdoors. The company's focus right now is a program called Get Dirty. REI has put together an employee volunteer program, through VolunteerMatch.com, that gets employees out of the store and into the local environmental doing cleanup projects at parks, beaches, and other outdoor recreation places. According to the company, in 2007 REI spent $3.5 million for outdoor recreation programs and stewardship projects, in the process helping care for recreational areas while introducing people to the outdoors, which, by the way, REI sells the equipment to help people enjoy. The campaign is effective branding for REI as a company, advertising for REI products, and CSR.

In its customer newsletter, REI now ask its customers to get involved on particular Get Dirty days in their areas. This is where REI employees team up with REI customers to take on local environmental projects. The message is simple and direct: we care about the environment, and we would like you to join us in helping to preserve it. For many people, this is a very compelling message—one that will bind them even more closely to REI and can lead to increased customer loyalty and increased sales for REI.

Summary

In today's world of 24/7 connectivity, overscheduling, self-absorption, multitasking, and barrages of brand noise and messaging, simplicity has never been more critical. The need for simplicity, in combination with the lack of a long history of CSR communications, means that messaging around concepts like carbon sequestration, five-step recycling programs, data center optimization, and fair-trade pricing simply cannot work. Stakeholders are not ready for these concepts, and they may never be willing to spend the time it will take to get educated enough to understand them.

CSR messaging needs to be simple: buy this bag of Pedigree, and help us help dogs. The cause needs to be clearly and simply aligned with the brand. The cause needs to be clear and understandable to even the most CSR focused of consumers (the Millennials). And the stakeholder needs to be engaged and called to action quickly and efficiently. There are a few brilliant examples of CSR communications that do these things, but the majority of CSR communications are still too long, lack clarity, are ill-defined and ill-fitting, or use legally disclaimed and obfuscated language. Your company has the power to brand your CSR in a way that is simple, direct, and understandable. Use it!

7

WORK FROM THE INSIDE OUT

There is more to the human condition than making money.
—Muhammad Yunus

Minneapolis-based Medtronic is one of the nation's largest manufacturers of implantable biomedical devices such as neurostimulators, heart pacemakers, and defibrillators. With more than $11 billion in annual sales in 2007, Medtronic was ranked number 222 on the Fortune 500.[33] A senior regional sales manager from Medtronic told me that, like many companies, Medtronic conducts annual sales meetings, often at five-star resorts in far-off exotic tropical locales. According to the manager, the purpose of these sales meetings was threefold: to reward the company's top salespeople, to get sales leaders from different regions together so they could leverage off one another and sell more Medtronic products, and to increase employee motivation and satisfaction with the company. One such meeting provides an example of how companies can engage their employees in their CSR programs.

Each year Medtronic rotates responsibility for planning and running its annual sales meetings among the company's regional sales managers. One year, it was this regional sales manager's turn to plan the meeting, and he decided to try something different—something that wouldn't involve five-star resorts, rounds of golf, and excessive food and alcohol intake. First, he went out and bought one hundred bikes at the local Toys "R" Us—unassembled, as toys so frustratingly are when purchased there, and still in their boxes. Next, he found a large ballroom in a local hotel and had all one hundred bikes delivered. Finally, when the meeting began, he got his sales folks together, put them into teams, and gave each team a pile of boxed and unassembled bikes. He told them that they were going to embark on a team-building exercise and that their job was simply to build as many workable, functioning bikes as possible in the time allotted.

Simple enough. The teams were full of type A, highly motivated, highly competitive salespeople who wanted to win.

The timer went off, and the sales teams all set about building their bikes. Some minutes later, the timer rang, and Medtronics' CEO strode into the room along with the regional sales manager in charge of the meeting. They walked down the lines of assembled bikes and inspected them closely to see if they were functioning—the pedals turned, and was the seat stable—and tallied the ones that met the standard. When they were about halfway through checking the bikes, the CEO said, "You know what, what do we know about bikes?"

Suddenly, the ballroom curtains opened, and one hundred kids from the local Boys and Girls Club came running out—mesmerized by the sight of one hundred shiny new bikes. The salespeople gave a newly assembled bike to each kid, and the kids excitedly rode them around the ballroom. For many, it was the first time they'd ever had their own bike, much less received such a gift from *anyone.* The manager told me, "You know what? I've been to fifteen-plus sales meetings, and I have never seen such an impact as it had on these employees. There were grown men sitting on the floor crying while they watched these kids who had never had anything like that of their own."

This is a great example of the power of corporate social responsibility and taking something that had been routine in the company and doing it slightly differently. The event met all of the company's goals for its annual sales meeting: It brought the salespeople together and involved team building. It was motivational and was rewarding for the men and women who participated in it. The cost, however, was just one-fifth what it would have been if they had gone to a five-star resort with the golf, the alcohol, and the food. And the satisfaction ratings were sky-high. Some of the Medtronic sales folks continue to volunteer with their local Boys and Girls Clubs, too. And this regional sales manager became a rock star within the company.

It's an Inside Job

Most companies that are deeply engaged in corporate social responsibility as a strategy have arrived there from a point of pain. Someone somewhere has criticized the company about something it has done or has failed to do, and usually that someone is on the outside. It can be an NGO, a watchdog or consumer group, a government regulator, or a competitor that's out to get the company. The pain the company experienced from one or more of these external stimuli has catapulted it into action. As I said earlier, pain is one of the fastest activators—for companies just as it is for individuals—and can be good because it forces those who lead a company to address the issue.

The process usually works like this: First, a small group from the company will engage with the external group that's causing them pain and talk through the issues. Next, the group will go back into the company, and this small group of employees will develop a fantastic strategy to satisfy that external group and relieve the pain point. However, many companies forget to do one thing during this process: engage internally with their own employee base. So they end up with a situation like the one I mentioned in chapter 5 where the barista at Starbucks didn't know anything about the Ethos Water for sale in the store. Starbucks had spent a lot of money purchasing Ethos and getting out the word about Ethos' mission of providing clean drinking water to the developing world—actions possibly linked to the fact that Starbucks' products, which are sold all around the world, are heavily water intensive. Starbucks even had a beautifully executed display in the store that provided customers with information about Ethos Water and for what it stands. But ask a random Starbucks employee what Ethos stands for, and all you might get back in return is a blank stare.

Why do companies overlook engaging their own employees in their CSR strategies and efforts? I believe there are a couple of key reasons. A company like Gap or McDonald's or Starbucks has such a high level of turnover within its retail workforce that it presumes it's too difficult—the company unfurls the white flag and gives up before the battle even starts. Or it presumes that employees just want to come in and get their jobs done and not get involved with such concerns as CSR. However, for a host of reasons it's a bad idea to neglect involving employees in your CSR programs.

Study after study shows that CSR is significantly linked to employee satisfaction. Employees tend to feel good about coming to work and earning a paycheck, as well as about contributing to some sort of a social or environmental issue. They become more loyal to the firm and often have better solutions than management does in tackling that social or environmental issue because they are on the frontlines. They're dealing with consumers and hearing a lot more about the issues customers are concerned about. For a company like Starbucks, the issue might be things like low wages for coffee harvesters or whether or not you really need the cardboard cup slipcover to keep your hands from getting burned.

Not getting employees involved is another missed opportunity—not just to communicate your CSR efforts but to engage employees and give them a chance to contribute to your business. As hard as it is to imagine, nine out of ten companies don't get employees involved. They intentionally or accidentally don't think about ways in which they can engage their own workforce. Doing so, however, is powerful on so many different levels—attracting the best talent, retaining talent, and keeping employees engaged and motivated. You can make your employees feel better about working for your company by getting them involved in your CSR program.

Although many employees are concerned (or at least interested) in the kinds of issues that make up external CSR—the environment, social issues, and human rights—another set of issues makes up internal CSR. As Table 1 shows, these items include diversity, health and wellness, and work-life balance. If your goal is to create an energized and engaged

Table 1. Internal and External CSR

Internal CSR	External CSR
Governance	Supply chain
Mission, vision, and values	Environment
Compensation and benefits	Human rights
Ethics	Philanthropy
Diversity	Community involvement and investment
Privacy (employee)	Transparency
Health and wellness	Reporting
Dependent care	Stakeholder engagement
Downsizing and layoffs	Sociopolitical issues
Work-life balance	Accountability
Job satisfaction	Privacy
	Marketplace

workforce (as it should be), then involving employees in both sides of your company's CSR story—internal and external—is essential.

Creating Employee Brand Ambassadors

One of the best things you can do to brand and communicate your CSR message is to create a cadre of internal employee brand ambassadors. Why? Because they're much more believable than that commercial you're going to spend $1 million producing and $2.4 million running on prime-time television. To get credible information on a company's CSR performance, people often seek word-of-mouth recommendations from people just like them. And your employees can be the ones to deliver some of that word-of-mouth messaging. It's a lot less expensive than running a full-page ad in the *New York Times,* and it's a whole lot more believable.

Nike is a company that has gotten its employees engaged internally perhaps as deeply as anyone, and maybe more. It had to, as it was involved in a lawsuit (*Kasky v. Nike*) for eighteen months, which thrust the company

RECRUITING HEWLETT-PACKARD'S NEW BRAND AMBASSADORS

Hewlett-Packard has recently embarked on a campaign to recruit an entirely new group of brand ambassadors: its retirees. In March 2008 Michael Mendenhall—chief marketing officer of Hewlett-Packard—attended the company's annual retiree meeting to urge the five hundred gathered former employees, along with hundreds more monitoring the proceedings over the Internet, to act as ambassadors for the company by joining local alumni clubs, speaking up on legislative issues Hewlett-Packard cares about, volunteering as salespeople, and representing the company in philanthropic and community events. In doing so, the company is tapping into a passionate group of company cheerleaders. Says Mendenhall, "We're moving forward with an effort to capitalize on the fact that we have these great brand stewards. When you look at the importance of great word of mouth and great third-party endorsement—who better to do that than your own employees?" The retirees seem to agree. According to ninety-one-year-old former HP customer service manager Chuck Ernst, "HP wants us to feel connected, and they're doing all this work to keep us connected. We're proud of the company, and we don't hesitate to let people know it."[34]

into a period of CSR silence. It developed a cross-functional employee CSR council. The council developed a strategy that it called spheres of influence, in which it created pockets of CSR influence inside the company and developed CSR champions in each part of those spheres to educate the sphere about the factory, compliance, policies, and more. Nike ended up developing a cadre of 160,000 brand ambassadors, which is a powerful force.

A Three-Step Process for Working from the Inside Out

Are you interested in engaging your employees in your CSR effort? If so, here are three steps for doing just that.

First, look for opportunities to build CSR into your employee training and development programs. You already have these programs anyway, so it is easy to add a CSR element to them. It's like giving your employees a drug. They'll feel loyal, satisfied, and identified with your company because they're getting an opportunity to talk about issues of corporate responsibility on the job and in training. They then go back to their departments where they can think about how to do things differently. For example, they can come up with ideas for weaving CSR topics into their next annual sales meeting, or what would happen if you took the light bulbs out of company break-room vending machines. But the first thing is to look for opportunities to build this into employee education in training and development programs.

Second, look for across-the-board opportunities to engage employees in your CSR efforts. You can engage employees by weaving CSR into employee performance appraisals. So, for example, Dow Chemical has a three-pronged corporate strategy comprising technology, innovation, and sustainability. You should see in its performance appraisal system employees being rated on the amount to which they've contributed to that three-pronged strategy, including sustainability. Remember the old adage that what gets measured gets done, and build CSR into your performance metrics. You'll quickly galvanize employees into action and improve your CSR strategy and its impact.

Third, develop the same level of consistent messaging across all of your marketing touchpoints. Most companies know all about messaging to consumers, but you should be strategically managing and sending the same messages to your employees too. Indeed, some companies are now realizing the power of utilizing CSR messaging in the employment process, particularly in attracting today's talent, because the generation of youth coming into the workforce, the Millennials, cares so much about doing business responsibly and being a part of the solution, not the problem. But you've got to be careful. There's nothing worse than an applicant hearing about all the great things you're doing with CSR during the recruitment process and then coming on as a sales analyst or a financial analyst or a brand manager and never being given the chance to engage with the company's CSR function.

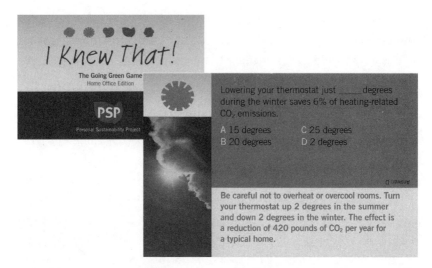

FIGURE 10. Wal-Mart's PSP card game (Wal-Mart Personal Sustainability Project, *The Going Green Game* [Bentonville, AR: Wal-Mart]).

One of the things that Wal-Mart did when it made its public commitment to reduce its own waste by 100 percent was to hold an internal employee competition to see who could come up with the best ideas to achieve this goal. They also developed the PSP (Personal Sustainability Program), which is a fun-looking, inviting card game (see Figure 10). Every one of Wal-Mart's employees was given the Going Green Game deck of cards, each of which has on it a sustainability question with multiple-choice answers from which the employee can choose.

It was this card game that led to the employee's idea to turn off all vending machine lights, as recounted in the Introduction. Unplugging all those light bulbs throughout the company has led to a savings of more than $1 million a year. And just imagine how good that employee feels because not only was he asked for his opinion, but he came up with a solution that had tremendous positive impact on the company's bottom line. This is employee engagement, training, and development at its best.

Wal-Mart has become effective at working from the inside out by using its already well-developed internal communications channels. The company is walking its talk: telling employees what it cares about and then

WE ARE NOT GREEN (YET)

You know that it's serious when the largest company in the world—Wal-Mart—decides to jump on the CSR bandwagon in a big way. And while its sincerity in going green has been questioned by some critics, Wal-Mart no doubt wouldn't be traveling down this road quite so wholeheartedly and rapidly if there weren't cost advantages to be gained in tandem with reducing the negative impact of its operations on the environment. In October 2005 Wal-Mart committed to three large sustainability goals:

- To be supplied 100 percent by renewable energy
- To create zero waste
- To sell products that sustain our resources and the environment.[35]

Wal-Mart has set the bar high, but it has not set arbitrary deadlines for attaining these goals. Instead, the company closely monitors its progress and will no doubt be in a state of becoming for many years. In fact, when asked at the *Wall Street Journal*'s ECO:nomics conference on the environment and business on March 13, 2008, when the company would meet its goals of being supplied 100 percent by renewable energy and having zero waste, Wal-Mart CEO Lee Scott Jr. replied, "I haven't a clue."[36] Scott went on to explain that the company was pursuing CSR not only to please environmentalists and other Wal-Mart critics but to save money. As he pointed out, with today's challenging economic environment, there is an even greater need to squeeze costs out of the system—now. Asked Scott, "When is a better time?"

rewarding employees who follow through and do the kinds of things that support what it cares about.

Up the Organization

It's natural to think about taking CSR messages *down* to your employees, but it's also important to think about taking them *up* through the executive team and board. When Gap was looking at its supply chain—and particularly at some issues it was having with its manufacturing in China—the company took its board of directors to China to experience the manufacturing environment firsthand. Dan Henkle, the vice president of CSR, arranged to have the board members taken through factories and shown the difficulties and the complexities of factory conditions and codes of conduct and having a factory where Gap was not the sole sourcer. In one factory, six different apparel companies were having products manufactured. The board was then shown the challenges of having six different codes of conduct on the walls.

Part of the reason for this field trip was because Gap's management was going to ask for a significant commitment from the company to develop a Gap supplier code of conduct and to develop a team of Gap auditors (in 2008 more than ninety strong) whose sole job it is to travel the globe auditing the factories from which the company sources. Until the board understood the need, it was hard to argue the need to maintain that high level of commitment. So while it's generally easy to engage downward to co-workers, don't forget to engage upward to the board too.

Levi Strauss & Company has four core values—empathy, originality, integrity, and courage—that are an elemental part of the company's DNA. You see this set of values throughout the company. It's part of the company's performance appraisals: How has this person performed with integrity? How has this person performed with courage? However, these values don't apply just down through the organization, from top to bottom; they also apply from the bottom up. Employees tend to do what they get measured to do on their performance appraisals, so if senior management makes the claim that values matter, it would make sense to measure employees on how well they meet those values in their work. CSR efforts often start from the top of a company, because the CEO believes in a cause or because the company is targeted by an activist group. CSR efforts also often start from the grassroots, because groups of engaged employees at the lower level make it happen. However, sometimes it's hardest to penetrate into the middle levels of the company. That's where you need to have consistent messaging at every touchpoint. Medtronic's sales meeting described at the beginning of this chapter is a brilliant example of bringing CSR to the middle ranks of the company.

Practice What You Preach

Conceptus, Inc., a fast-growing, highly successful company that is engaged in the design, development, and marketing of innovative medical products for women, came to Haas School of Business and me for some executive education. We discussed the need for a CSR strategy, which in this case was rich with opportunity because the company's chosen focus was the "empowerment of women." We began to explore partnerships with women's health clinics and women's educational organizations. The possibilities were endless, and the participating employees were quickly becoming excited by them. Suddenly, one female employee urgently raised her hand. "How can we," she asked, "develop this deep value statement and CSR strategy around the empowerment of women and offering birth control choice to women globally when we as a company do not even cover birth control for our own employees under our corporate health care program?"

This shortcoming might sound minor to some, while seeming egregious to others. What is most surprising is that it is a common scenario. Companies go to great lengths to create CSR programs that are focused *externally,* for stakeholders outside their corporate walls. And yet they fail to focus their CSR internally and engage their largest and most valuable asset (and, coincidentally, their best brand ambassadors)—their employees. The reason for this is actually quite simple: many organizations have an impenetrable wall separating all things internal within the company from all things external. Having an externally focused CSR program comes about when companies are pushed (sometimes screaming) into the world of CSR in response to some sort of external stimulus or pressure that becomes public, often embarrassing and painful, and that threatens brand and image.

In the case of Conceptus, the medical products company was in the favorable position of not having to respond (yet) to external public pres-

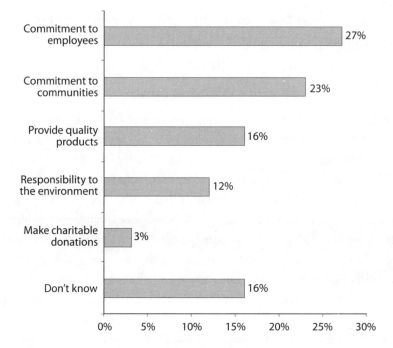

FIGURE 11. What is the meaning of "corporate social responsibility"? (Fleishman-Hillard and National Consumers League, *Rethinking Corporate Social Responsibility*, CSR Survey 07, http://www.csrresults.com/).

sure. It wasn't feeling pain and was therefore not being forced into a reactive mode. Companies that are not yet under external public pressure are in a particularly good place to design a forward-looking framework for focusing their CSR programs internally and for engaging and involving employees, both in program design and ongoing execution.

The old saying "charity begins at home" does apply when it comes to CSR. Take care of your own house first. Would you be surprised to learn that many people believe that socially responsible companies should take care of their employees first, before saving the world? When companies focus their CSR programs externally and neglect their internal component of CSR, employees rightfully wonder why *they* don't count as importantly as the chosen cause, whether it is saving polar bears in the Arctic, honeybees in Bakersfield, or malaria victims in Africa. A 2006 Fleishman-Hillard/National Consumers League study asked people to define *corporate social responsibility* (see Figure 11). The results of this study show that at the very top of the list of things that make up CSR was "commitment to employees." In second place was "commitment to communities," and "responsibility to the environment" was farther down the list in fourth place.

The results are the same when people around the globe are asked about the meaning of corporate social responsibility. It does not matter where people come from—they define CSR first as taking care of workers.[37]

Ecomagination Goes Internal

Can a CSR strategy help an old-line multinational conglomerate remain a powerhouse in the twenty-first century while turning being green (social responsibility) into green (cash)? If you consider the example of General Electric—number six on the Fortune 500 list, with annual revenues of more than $168 billion in 2007—and its Ecomagination strategy, the answer is an unequivocal yes.[38]

According to General Electric chairman and CEO Jeffrey Immelt, "Ecomagination is GE's commitment to address challenges such as the need for cleaner, more efficient sources of energy, reduced emissions, and abundant sources of clean water."[39] On its Web site, GE says that at the heart of Ecomagination are four commitments: (1) double investments in clean research and development, (2) increase revenues from Ecomagination products, (3) reduce greenhouse gas emissions, and (4) keep the public informed. Three years into its Ecomagination strategy, the company has begun to realize some real benefits.

GE's investment in research in clean technologies will grow from $900 million in 2006 to $1.5 billion by 2010. And GE has made money with Ecomagination—revenues surpassed $12 billion in 2006 (up 20 percent from the previous year) and are on track to jump past $20 billion in 2010.[40] However, the benefits that GE has realized internally from Ecomagination to date have turned out to be far more important than the company ever anticipated.

One of the most significant challenges that GE faces is that the company is really a collection of disparate business units. There are units in the business of health care, finance, consumer goods, capital, aircraft, and more. The problem is that these units are all separate from one another, or "siloed," so it's difficult to get the managers at the different units to talk to one another, let alone understand the business models. The company's corporate management is constantly trying to find ways to get people to reach out across these business-line silos and create more opportunities to work together and cross-sell one another's products.

Corporate leaders tried all kinds of initiatives and spent lots of money trying to bust employees out of their silos with limited success, but they began to notice something interesting. GE's Ecomagination strategy—designed to increase the energy efficiency of GE's operations and products, thereby improving the environment as well as making GE money—was itself having an impact on employee behavior. Employees were becoming energized by the idea that they could do their jobs—say, product marketing, or R&D—and at the same time contribute to a better environment and a better world. People in different GE divisions started to talk to one another, reaching out across the silos. For the first time, GE aircraft employees began cross-selling their clients on GE health care, and GE health care employees began cross-selling their clients on GE financial services. As it turned out, GE's CSR program turned out to be one of the highest-impact internal unification strategies that the company has ever implemented—an outcome that was unexpected and not part of the initial intent. Corporate leaders were unaware of the power of CSR to be a unifying force for employees. Again, CSR can be like a drug for employees, in a great, healing, motivating way.

Levi Strauss's Internal Fabric

Earlier in this chapter, we considered Levi Strauss & Company's four core values—empathy, originality, integrity, and courage. When you talk to anybody at Levi Strauss—from brand manager to store manager to the person who is running the company's supply chain—you'll hear that those four words mean a lot to them. The values are such a part of their internal fabric that anytime employees make a key business decision, or pitch a client in hopes of a major sale, or make a major business move, they filter their decision-making process through these principles. They first ask themselves, "Does this approach represent integrity, originality, courage, empathy?" If it doesn't fit with these principles, they go back to the drawing board and try again.

Most large companies have a corporate foundation, and Levi Strauss does too. However, the approach Levi Strauss took with its foundation is unique, and it reflects the company's core values. In 1981, former Levi Strauss marketing executive Jerry O'Shea and his wife Claire launched the Red Tab Foundation, contributing $100,000 of their own funds to kick it off. According to Levi Strauss' Web site, the Red Tab Foundation is a 501(c)(3) nonprofit that exists under Levi Strauss's auspices but that is funded exclusively by employees, run exclusively by employees, and exists exclusively to assist Levi Strauss employees and retirees who are unable to pay for life's basic necessities due to unexpected emergencies.

Membership on the Red Tab Foundation board of directors rotates among Levi Strauss employees, who review the grant requests, make funding decisions, and then personally deliver the check to the company employee or retiree. The foundation has a DVD that serves as an internal marketing piece, and it is high impact. In the DVD, recipients of Red Tab Foundation grants tell their stories. One story is told by an elderly woman in New York who had been a sewer for Levi Strauss her entire life and had been retired from the company for more than fifteen years. She lived in a small rent controlled apartment in New York City, and she had lost the use of her legs and needed to use a wheelchair to get around. Unfortunately, she could no longer use the bathroom in her own apartment, and she was living on a fixed income and didn't have the means to pay the cost of retrofitting her bathroom with hand bars and wheelchair ramps so she would be able to use it. She applied for and was granted a Red Tab Foundation grant to retrofit her bathroom. As she gratefully says in the video, "You know, I gave this company my life. And you know what, this company just gave me back my life."

The Red Tab Foundation has touched many other lives. There's the Levi Strauss retail store employee whose apartment building caught fire. He lost everything so he needed money simply to get into a new place to live. And there was a white-collar worker in San Francisco whose husband left her and her son. She needed help to be able to continue to pay the tuition for her son during the divorce proceedings so the boy could continue in school. Levi Strauss does a lot of good things around the world, but through the Red Tab Foundation, it shows employees that *they* come first. The company knows that CSR starts with taking care of your workers.

The Transformation of Timberland's Board

In 1989 clothing manufacturer Timberland developed a deep partnership with City Year, a nonprofit that unites young people of all backgrounds for a year of full-time service to the community, giving them skills and opportunities to change the world. The partnership has been a good one for both organizations. Timberland gets brand leverage, and City Year receives funding, warm coats, waterproof boots, and other resources from the company. It's no coincidence that City Year volunteers wear bright red jackets produced by and cobranded with Timberland.

At some point during the development of this relationship, Timberland CEO Jeff Swartz was invited to join City Year's board of directors. Swartz already had a CSR program at Timberland, which was one of the first to grant forty hours a year of paid time off for its employees to volunteer in their communities. During the course of one of City Year's board meetings, a thought occurred to him: "I run a company. I have a strong social mission, but when I sit in my board meetings with my own board all we talk about are the financial aspects of this company." That particular circumstance would soon change.

Swartz invited Billy Shore—founder and executive director of Share Our Strength, a successful Washington, D.C.–based nonprofit that works with hunger and homelessness—to join the Timberland board. However, Shore's role on the board was to be quite different from the traditional financial one. His sole responsibility was to watch over Timberland's social mission, and he remains on the board to this day. Although this transformation of the normal role of the board was groundbreaking, other companies, including Whole Foods, are emulating Timberland's example.

The Gapateria and Other Employee Pursuits

If you ever have business at Gap's corporate headquarters at Two Folsom Street in San Francisco, you might go to the company's cafeteria, which is affectionately referred to as the Gapateria by employees. As you look around the Gapateria, you will see signs encouraging employees to think about the environment when they make their meal decisions. For example, signs remind employees who are going to grab lunch and take it back to their offices to take it on a reusable glass plate instead of a Styrofoam box, and to toss their recyclables into the proper bin.

There are also copies of Gap's excellent six-page *Corporate Citizenship at Gap* report available for employees to peruse while they're eating their meals. This report is aimed solely at employees, and it clearly spells out what company employees do in corporate social responsibility efforts, from serving on boards of nonprofits to volunteering in the community to raising money for causes. By having this report right by all of the tables, the company gives employees the opportunity to find out what good things the company is doing in the world—including its work with Product Red. And speaking of Product Red, employees have demonstrated their support for this initiative by giving up their normal employee discount on Product Red products so the proceeds go to support the fight against AIDS in Africa.

Summary

Your company's employees, whether they are 1,000 or 160,000 in number, are your most valuable CSR asset. Engage them, involve them, and include them in your CSR strategy. Develop cross-functional CSR councils to develop, refine, and monitor your CSR strategy. You will attract and retain the best talent. You will increase their satisfaction, motivation, and loyalty. You will create a cadre of enthusiastic brand ambassadors. And, like Wal-Mart, you might just get lucky and have an employee well-trained in CSR suggest an easy way to save the company over $1 million a year.

8

KNOW YOUR CUSTOMER

You cannot win the hearts of customers unless you have a heart yourself.
—Charlotte Beers, former advertising executive

I learned something significant about CSR and knowing your customers from the rapper Sean Combs (aka P. Diddy). I was invited to attend the Product Red launch at the Gap headquarters and was seated next to Bobby Shriver, who is Maria Shriver's brother and the cofounder, with Bono, of Product Red. At the time, I was doing some research looking at the relationship between diversity and corporate responsibility. Bobby Shriver was describing the difficulties they were having in getting companies to sign on to Product Red, and he mentioned American Express U.S. Apparently American Express Europe had signed on to Product Red, but the U.S. division felt much more hesitant about attaching its brand to AIDS and Africa. Shriver went on to describe how in the United States American Express's retail market penetration was predominantly white, male, middle-aged businessmen. The company was looking for ways to expand into new market segments, such as females and Hispanics.

As we talked, he was reminded of something Sean Combs said to him and Bono when they were soliciting him to do pro bono modeling for their Product Red campaign.

Apparently Bono and Shriver were meeting with Combs in his recording studio in Los Angeles and were pitching him on the impact Product

© iStock

Red could have on disease and AIDS in Africa, but for the campaign to be successful, they needed star power in their advertising. Halfway through their pitch, Combs looked straight at Bobby and straight at Bono and said, "Shut up. I am sick of hearing you guys talk, both of you!" (Can you imagine saying this to Bono?) He went on to warn them, "Do you know what you guys are? You are a couple of lions. And this campaign is doomed to failure with a bunch of lions running it. Do you know what lions do all day? They wake up, saunter out to the biggest shade tree, and they lie right back down and take a nap. Do you know what lionesses do all day? They wake up, hunt, kill, and gather the lion's lunch and bring it back to him—all the time keeping their den and watching over lots of little cubs!"

Combs warned Bono and Bobby to get the lionesses involved in Product Red, or it was doomed to failure. He advised them to involve lionesses like Mary J. Blige, Oprah, and Penelope Cruz. On October 13, 2006, Product Red launched on *The Oprah Winfrey Show*. Web traffic on the e-commerce sites of the five companies that then made up Product Red went up 2,600 percent during the hour following the Oprah launch. Are you using lionesses in your corporate social responsibility campaign?

Do You Know Your Customers?

Today's customers have increasingly become an enlightened lot. They are seeking to become educated about the socially responsible things their favorite companies are doing, and their expectations for the future are continually on the rise. A commitment to CSR is quickly on its way to becoming the norm instead of the exception, and people are beginning to respond with their loyalty—and their dollars—to companies that offer effective substance and communication. I do fear that the pendulum of responsibility may have swung so far that consumers now expect businesses to be completely responsible for all of the impacts of the choices that these consumers themselves make. Little attention is now given to *individual responsibility* and choice—such as the choice to buy that large, gas-guzzling sport-utility vehicle (SUV), build that monstrous energy-inefficient house, or eat five Big Macs—and plenty of attention is given to the "irresponsible" company that manufactured an offending product.

Even the most CSR-savvy consumer segments, Millennials and women, still need first to understand the impact of their socially responsible behavior on themselves, their health, and their wallets, before they take the next step of worrying about the Amazonian rain forest or working conditions in Indonesia. In general I have found that consumers tend to care about things that are "in me" (or in my kid), "on me" (or on my kid), or "around me" (or around my kid) first and foremost. CSR branding attributes need to start with those concerns, passing through the physical or cognitive corpus of the consumer first before reaching further afield to issues such as the Amazonian rain forest.

Think of consumer needs in terms of Maslow's pyramid (see Figure 12): people try to satisfy their needs for physiological basics, for safety, for love and belonging, for esteem, and for self-actualization.

Each layer of Maslow's pyramid can be linked to some aspect of CSR: providing and protecting clean drinking water and clean air; offering products free of harmful chemicals; belonging to a group that is doing good for the planet; being loved by formerly homeless animals that have been adopted into loving homes; and, finally, reaching your potential and making the world a better place through your spending and work-

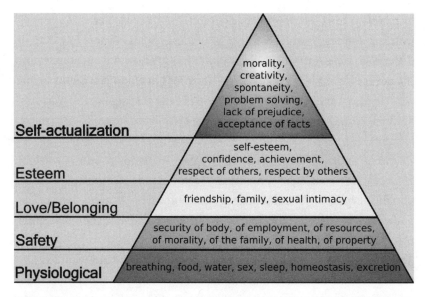

FIGURE 12. Maslow's pyramid (J. Finkelstein, "Maslow's Hierarchy of Needs," 2006, http://commons.wikimedia.org/wiki/Image:Maslow's_hierarchy_of_needs.svg).

ing choices. The opportunity here—not the challenge—is to link the CSR attributes of brand to what is in it for the individual, exactly as is done in traditional branding.

Better Messaging for Customers

Let's consider for a moment telling your CSR story in a way that is understandable and accessible to consumers. The British grocery and general merchandising retail chain Tesco is working with a British government organization called the Carbon Trust to try to accurately calculate the carbon footprint of every product that the company sells. These numbers will then be placed on the packaging for each of these products, allowing consumers to judge for themselves which items are truly best for the environment and emit the least amount of carbon into the air.[41]

Of course, as you would imagine in the case of something as contentious as climate change, and with the kinds of complex concepts and calculations involved in figuring carbon footprints, Tesco has gotten a lot of criticism over its attempt to do good. Much of this criticism comes from academicians and scientists who disagree about how to calculate the carbon emissions for each product. Exactly how do you start—from the point of growth of apples on the farm? What all do you factor in and out—the packaging, the petroleum used in the packaging, the transportation from farm to market? Calculating an accurate number is a mind-boggling task.

We can and always will disagree over the calculations—just as you look at a company's financial spreadsheet or government's budget and question the accuracy of the numbers. I don't know why presentations of carbon emissions or other CSR metrics have to be detailed to the nth decimal place when we know fully well that few others metrics are. Consumers don't care about these details, which to them are trivia. They want to know the big picture. Is what you are doing good for the environment or bad? And how can choices be made based on this factor, as well as on the traditional consumer choice factors of price, quality, and convenience? How can consumers add this fourth factor into their decision-making mix?

Tesco has decided to place a symbol of an airplane on packages that are transported by air from farm to market. This symbol will differentiate such products from locally produced ones that will not have airplane symbols. Few consumers really want to work through the complexities of calculating a carbon footprint, or to argue whether the impact is 2 kilograms of carbon versus 3 kilograms. A simple symbol is really all they need and want, and if it is 80 percent accurate, that is fine. If I can choose to buy apples with an airplane symbol and know that they were flown in from some faraway place versus apples that were grown just two hours away and that were transported by truck, then I know all I need to know as a consumer. Even with an 80 percent accuracy rate, I can understand that apples from Africa have used more carbon than apples from Manchester. The science doesn't have to be exact for my purposes.

The LOHAS Effect

The Natural Marketing Institute coined the phrase "lifestyles of health and sustainability" (LOHAS) as a new and growing customer segment that generally cuts across socioeconomic status and even gender. It tends to be made up of highly educated, middle- to upper-middle-class people interested in sustainability and green initiatives. Amy Cortese of the *New York Times* remarked that the LOHAS market segment is perhaps the largest group of consumers that you've never heard of.[42]

According to the Natural Marketing Institute's information on customer segmentation and of all the different market segments that it tracks, LOHAS is the only market segment that has been continuously growing over the past ten years, with the heaviest growth in the past three years. When I first started tracking this data in the late 1990s, about 9 percent of consumers were in the LOHAS segment. Today, the number has grown to about 30 percent of consumers.[43] A number of factors have spurred this growth, including a desire to be healthy, fit, and active; the sharply increased cost of gasoline and other energy sources; the war in Iraq; increasing knowledge and concern over environmental degradation; and fears of global warming.

Companies trying to use their advertising dollars as efficiently and effectively as possible need to know as much as they can about consumers and their shopping preferences relative to society and the environment. However, the majority of companies are obviously not doing a very good job of capturing this sort of data. Many companies are starting to see the benefit of offering new products to this segment. Even Clorox has gotten into the act with its new environmentally friendly cleaning line called Green Works, undoubtedly designed to compete with the highly successful Method Products brand. When industry heavyweights like Clorox get into the act, you've got to believe that they've checked with their customers, and their customers have spoken: we want to buy green.

Some Customers Are Ready, and Some Aren't

It astounds me that we are criticizing any company that's trying to do the right thing. At least give Tesco some credit for attempting it. Is it a perfect science? No. Will the science get better over time? Absolutely. So part of what companies need to do is to get their CSR message out in a way in which the consumer feels empowered, so the consumer has a choice—to buy a low-emissions apple rather than the high-emissions apple that has been shipped by air. Companies can also start with ready consumer markets, and some consumer segments are more ready than others.

Millennials

Certainly the Millennial generation—people between the ages of eight and thirty—have shown they deeply care about, and will act upon, these issues. They overwhelmingly respond that they feel the world is going in a negative direction, and they feel personally responsible to change the direction. And they feel not only personally responsible but personally empowered to create change. They want to use both their buying power and their careers to support companies that are on that same trajectory toward making the world a better place.

One study, the 2006 Cone Millennial Cause Study, found that 89 percent of Millennials, or members of Generation Y, would switch brands if that brand was linked to a cause and they *knew* about it. Nearly 80 percent of these Millennials want to work for a company that cares about society and is contributing positively to it. And nearly 75 percent of this group will pay attention to a company's messaging if the company is doing more than simply trying to sell them something—if the message shows a deep commitment to improving the world.

Again, Millennials are those people between the ages of eight and thirty in 2008. So you might argue that they do not own the power of the purse in terms of sheer dollar power. But to anyone who has a Millennial or two in the household, you have surely found, as have I, that even with no dollars in their pocket or purse they significantly control (and spend) the dollars in my purse. And if you are not trying to attract Millennials as customers, you are trying to attract this group as your employees—this is, for the most part, who you are hiring in the job market. So remember, when getting out your brand message, speak to your consumers and to your potential employee talent.

The Lioness Factor

The other segment of the market that may care about CSR issues is females. If that is the case for Tesco, where you would reckon over 80 percent of its customer base is probably women, getting out its CSR message makes a lot of sense. I set out to have a closer look at the data.

I found that women are more likely than men are to investigate an organization's environmental and social performance before joining, investing, or making a purchase. Consider Net Impact, the national organization of MBA students and alumni who are committed to using the power of business to change the world. Even though according to the Graduate Management Admission Council only 25 percent of students in MBA programs are women, Net Impact's membership is 60 percent women, so in this aspect of business, women are overrepresented. In each of the fifty states, women are more likely than men to volunteer in their communities. Women are more likely to purchase a product if a percentage of the sale price goes toward a cause that they care about. Women are more likely than men to review their investment portfolio for environmental and social performance as well as financial return. And when I looked at a few internal company CSR initiatives aimed at employees, women were more likely to sign up, commit, and participate. So if you want to speak to the power of the purse, or if you want to attract and retain top female employee talent (remember, your employees are your customers, too, and need to be branded to and engaged), use your CSR substance.

Goldman Sachs applied this knowledge of the empowerment of women in 2008 when it announced its 10,000 Women campaign. This venerable investment bank, a leader in the industry, understands that the health and wealth of entire nations rests on the educational level, health, and engagement of their female citizens. Dubbing it "womenomics," Goldman Sachs found that educating girls and women in developing countries leads to higher wages, greater likelihood of working outside the home, lower rates of maternal and child mortality, and hence higher productivity in the country. Goldman Sachs has committed $100 million over five years to the campaign, and the company is engaging its employees to help in the effort to educate over ten thousand women from the developing world in business acumen and skills.

Stealth CSR

Many companies have aspects of social responsibility as a part of their corporate strategy. However, these same companies may not mention CSR in their product offerings or messaging, or mention that they put out products that are more environmentally friendly. I mentioned earlier the example of Dreyer's ice cream and how it kept quiet about the fact that its cartons were made of recycled paper. For five years, the company was utilizing 30 percent postconsumer paper in its cartons and wasn't advertising the fact anywhere in its promotional materials or product packaging. Today, Dreyer's uses 80 percent postconsumer paper in its cartons, and it still isn't advertising this fact or attaching it to its brand. Dreyer's is missing out on a lot of great opportunities to communicate this aspect of its CSR program.

So why not communicate CSR to consumers? At least part of the reason is that companies believe they know their customers well, and they believe their customers don't care about CSR. The common belief is that consumers care only about the price and quality of the products they buy. I'm not sure that we've fully tested that theory. Consumers know the price of a product; it is easy to see. And they can quickly find reports on the quality of the product, or read about it on the product's own advertising or packaging.

I met with executives at Tiffany & Company, the jewelry retailer headquartered in New York City. We were discussing a program that the company has been involved in for six years with a nonprofit by the name of SeaWeb. The program focuses on keeping coral in the ocean for its positive impact on the ecosystem, and six years ago Tiffany stopped selling coral jewelry in its stores. We also talked about the issue of conflict diamonds and how Tiffany was one of the first companies to implement an anti-conflict-diamond supply chain. In passing the CSR manager from Tiffany said to me, "I've got to be honest, our consumers aren't asking about the anti-conflict-zone sourcing of our diamonds. They don't come in when they are shopping for an engagement ring and say, I want X quality, Y size, and Z clarity, and also I don't want it to be a conflict diamond."

I said, "I get that, but I think at some level Tiffany exists to educate consumers. You have a proactive diamond-quality educational program. I didn't know, for example, that diamonds come in different colors. You have no problem educating me on that, so why wouldn't you educate me on the fact that nobody's limbs were lost or no eleven-year-olds were killed to sell me that diamond?" A common thought is that companies that rest their brands on being high quality, high price-point tend to view

CSR as somehow counter to those brand attributes. I believe that this is not true, or at least it is untested.

The excuse I often get for a company's decision not to communicate its CSR message is "But my customers don't care; they aren't asking for it." I get frustrated with repeatedly getting this assertion. Companies are always leading consumers in terms of needs and wants. I don't know too many consumers who felt they needed a 360-degree swivel toothbrush complete with thirty days' worth of toothpaste in its base, yet Oral-B tells me I do. And I do not know of too many women who wanted their mates to sustain an eight-hour erection, yet Viagra, from Pfizer, has the ability to deliver that want.

So why can't companies help to create the desires and needs for socially responsible products and services?

In the case of Tiffany, a socially responsible message may get potential customers in the door. Sure, once they get in the door, they may not ask about whether or not a diamond is conflict free. They may see an ad in the *New York Times* that mentions the anti-conflict-diamond policy, and it gets them in the door, and then they ask about color, clarity, carats, and so forth (*conflict-free* could be the fifth "c" in diamond buying!). The message differentiates Tiffany from the rest of the competition.

Many people feel intimidated to walk into Tiffany because the stores can appear to have an air of superiority. If Tiffany talked about what it did to halt the loss of life in Africa over diamond mining, it might make the brand a little more approachable. It would surely give Tiffany a powerful, humanizing brand story and make me feel better about my two-carat diamond purchase. And I'd be sure to tell all of my girlfriends to buy their right-hand rings from Tiffany. I don't think mentioning a social angle detracts from consumers' perception of the diamond's quality if you brand it right. It brings Tiffany down to earth a little bit and shows that the company cares and that it's committed to things like fine jewelry and the lives of human beings.

We can make the assumption that customers would care if we communicated to them (1) in a way that they could understand the message and (2) in a way that pushed the message more proactively. Consumers need to first understand how something is good for them—why they should be concerned about AIDS in Africa, and why buying a particular product that generates a monetary contribution to fight AIDS will be something that's in their interest. Being in their interest could be as simple as making consumers feel better about a purchase—if they purchase diamond A versus diamond B, they're actually helping to save a life. Consumers need to understand in clear, simple terms what they are helping to do. Clearly, buying a diamond is not going to directly save a life, but you could certainly say that buying a conflict-free diamond is helping to save lives in Africa. It has to be that simple, that direct and straightforward.

Here's another example of the need for companies to admit that they can help to create the desire for socially responsible products and services. Vehicle owners are converting from SUVs or heavy trucks to light cars—primarily hybrids. The highest penetration rate for hybrid vehicles of anyplace in the nation is in San Francisco, but slightly over 80 percent of owners of hybrid vehicles in San Francisco also owned a second car, and this second car was an SUV. The highest conversion rates of people who had actually left their heavy trucks or SUVs and then purchased a hybrid were on military bases—military personnel buying a hybrid for their civilian car. The high rate makes sense because military personnel are on a fixed income and don't have a high disposable income. But surprisingly this high conversion rate on military bases has been accompanied by a similar increase in environmental philanthropy on military bases.

This increase in environmental philanthropy is despite the fact that Democrats are more likely to give philanthropically to environmental causes than Republicans, and military bases are more likely to be Republican than Democratic. However, because these people felt the pain first in their wallet, something near and dear to all of us, they bought more environmentally friendly cars, and they reaped the benefit of lower fuel costs. They then started to understand and feel good about contributing to the environment and doing something good for the earth by reducing the amount of CO_2 going into the atmosphere. But they had to feel it personally first.

People don't normally go directly from point A (driving a low-miles-per-gallon, high-polluting SUV) to point C (feeling good about making a positive contribution to the environment). They usually need to pass through point B first. In this case, point B was buying a hybrid car. Once they reap the benefits of visiting point B, they could then care more broadly about CO_2 emissions or rivers in the Amazon.

So that's the challenge for presenting your case to a consumer. Your pitch can't be solely and immediately about how buying your product will save lives in Africa, and it cannot be disconnected from the traditional branding attributes of price, quality, and convenience. You've got to include CSR and integrate it with price, quality, and convenience, and you've also got to explain to consumers what it does for them. Again, this can be as little as making them feel better or it can be as profound as saving money while you're helping the environment. "What's in it for me" has to come first.

When you think about what your customer segments are, and which customers are ready to hear what you've got to say, it may not make sense to roll out CSR messaging across the board on all of your products, and it may not make sense to put your CSR messaging out through all of your different outlets. Tesco has many different kinds of stores, including traditional grocery stores, superstores, and express convenience stores. In the United States, Tesco has a new brand of convenience store called Fresh & Easy, which is a little more upscale than the traditional UK-based Tesco. That is a market segment where it would make sense for Tesco to push more of its CSR message—its carbon labeling and its community work—because that's going to be more of a sweet spot in terms of its customer segment.

Another example of messaging to different outlets is when Gap partnered with Product Red. Gap made the partnership with the Gap brand as opposed to its more upscale Banana Republic brand. I wonder if Banana Republic might have been a better place to focus the message. In a way it's going to be a toss-up because Gap attracts more of the Millennials, while Banana Republic attracts a more upscale, older consumer with a higher level of disposable income. I'm not saying that Gap did or did not make the right decision but just that it may have left some opportunity on the table and might want to take another look at which brand would do the best job of generating money for Product Red. It's not just helping to combat AIDS in Africa; it is also about bringing the company business success. In any case, businesses need to go through the same exercises with their CSR messaging and branding that they do with their regular branding and messaging.

Supply-Chain Ambassadors

Another way to reach your company's customers with your CSR message is through your supply chains. For example, Wal-Mart uses its supply chain when it promotes General Electric and its Ecomagination strategy by giving GE's CFL light bulbs premium visibility inside the store. Wal-Mart also gave GE premium advertising by featuring the CFL light bulbs to over 200 million customers in its April 2008 *Earth Month* magalogue. This in-store magalogue educated and advertised to Wal-Mart shoppers the products that used less energy, produced less waste, or used fewer chemicals during production on the farm or in the factory.

Wal-Mart also can and should reach out to GE and ask it to become a brand ambassador for Wal-Mart and to help it get its CSR message out to a wider audience. Similarly, if Dow Chemical is supplying plastics to Hewlett-Packard for the manufacture of computers and printers, Dow Chemical can and should ask HP to help communicate Dow Chemical's commitment to social responsibility. HP could issue a press release or put something on its Web site saying, "We picked Dow Chemical's plastics because of its commitment to clean drinking water, and that's something that's near and dear to our hearts."

Knowing your customer applies just as much when you are talking about companies that sell directly to retail as it does to companies that are selling to other companies—business to business. If your company is trying to get on Hewlett-Packard's list of approved vendors and you know that CSR is part of its overall corporate strategy, you can use CSR as a way to differentiate your company when you make your pitch. HP and many other companies have a section in their vendor or supplier application forms for a supplier to discuss its own CSR strategy. And Wal-Mart is now active in pushing CSR down the supply chain. Wal-Mart does not want to be alone in making the commitment to reduce its packaging or energy use. It is requiring its vendors and suppliers to have the same kind of a commitment. These vendors get premium shelf space and product placement, which become a competitive advantage and a point of differentiation.

Summary

The old assumption that consumers do not care about CSR has simply not been adequately tested. My hypothesis is that we have not yet figured out how to *communicate* a company's CSR substance in a way that is as effective as the company's traditional branding and advertising. And workers are also consumers. We tend to think of people who purchase our products and services and brand only to them. We also need to brand our products and services to our employees, our suppliers, the governments, and communities in which we desire to do business, and to our investors. We are all, at some point in our lives, all of those things as well as consumers. CSR can be an effective branding strategy to many more groups than just consumers if communicated effectively.

9

TELL YOUR STORY

> A good story cannot be devised; it has to be distilled.
> —Raymond Chandler

If you are not yet convinced that effectively telling your CSR story, based on solid CSR substance, will have a positive impact on your company, read on. In April 2008 I led a CSR symposium in Haiti for local business leaders. The sponsor of the symposium was Digicel, which is an Irish-owned mobile telecommunications operator in the Caribbean and Central American markets run by Irishman Denis O'Brien. The company launched the Digicel Foundation in 2004 with the purpose of strengthening Caribbean communities. In Haiti, the poorest country in the Western Hemisphere, where the majority of the inhabitants live on less than a dollar a day, the foundation has made a commitment to youth, education, and sport and has been responsible for the building of over twenty schools.

In April 2008 food riots broke out in several parts of the world, including Haiti. The riots in Haiti occurred in the country's two largest cities, Les Caye and the capital of Port-au-Prince, and left six people dead and hundreds injured and led to the ouster of Prime Minister Jacques-Édouard Alexis. While I was in Port-au-Prince, I heard from envious Haitian business leaders about Digicel's deep commitment to the Haitian community. During the riots, hungry Haitian citizens threw bricks and burning rubber tires through storefronts and looted the stores for goods and cash in an effort to obtain food for their starving families; they also sent a message to these capitalistic companies that fundamental needs were left unmet in the country in which they were conducting business.

Amazingly, storefronts to the left and to the right of Digicel shops were shattered and ransacked, but the Digicel stores were left intact. Even more amazingly, the reason the Digicel stores were spared is not that the rioters intentionally left them alone. Haitian citizens who understood what Digicel had done for the country, not only by bringing the people access to affordable cell phones but also by building schools and by sponsoring the national soccer team, banded together in small community-policing groups and protected the Digicel stores. They viewed Digicel not simply as another capitalist company operating in Haiti only to make money but as a community contributor operating in Haiti's best interests, bettering Haitian society, and providing hope for this seemingly hopeless country.

So these Digicel customers protected Digicel store fronts from the bricks, burning tires, damage, and theft. Telling your CSR story has an impact on consumers even during times of starvation and street anarchy.

Also recall from chapter 5 the recruiting visits of McKinsey and Dow Chemical. McKinsey missed a branding opportunity by not preparing one of its senior of partners to tell its CSR story. Dow Chemical did not miss the opportunity to tell its story. In fact, the Dow Chemical team of senior managers presented the company's CSR program in the form of excerpts from Dow Chemical's recently launched Human Element brand campaign. This campaign is an effective mix of senior leadership vision, substance, actions, and marketing and branding collateral—all built around the company's CSR substance.

The "human element" represents a new "element" that Dow Chemical has "discovered" and figuratively placed on the element chart to illustrate what the company's products and good works are doing to improve the human condition. For example, it is bringing clean drinking water to those who need it through the company's water purification filters. The Haas students were abuzz in the days following Dow Chemical's recruiting presentation, and all four of Dow Chemical's offers were accepted. Clearly, Dow Chemical did a better job of telling its CSR story. Sadly, many companies have not even begun to develop the CSR strategy to lend substance to any CSR story.

The Risk of Telling Your Story (or Not)

As valuable as CSR is, it is not the panacea to all that ails companies—lousy products, overpriced services, poor branding, or inadequate customer segmentation—let alone all that ails the world. Similarly, I want to be clear that telling your story always holds some element of risk, although I would argue that the risk of telling your CSR story is likely significantly less than not telling your CSR story. But everything a company does has an element of risk, so why not be the one to craft your CSR story, instead of waiting for someone else to do it for you—in a way that is negative and such that you can neither control nor easily counter it?

First, you don't want to brand or communicate your CSR when there's no substance to back it up. In today's fast-track-to-information world, that would simply be stupid. The substance has to be there first; the story comes second.

No good deed goes unpunished. So as soon as a company like Tesco proudly announces that it has added one thousand new product lines since launching its local sourcing campaign a couple of years ago, some cynical blogger is complaining that the only reason the company did this was to cover up for something bad it's done previously. Regardless of what your CSR story is, it won't be long before some people will start digging deeper into it.

However, the majority of the companies I work with have the substance—year upon year of working on recycling and transparent reporting and supply-chain codes of conduct and energy efficiency—and they are reticent, or scared stiff, to communicate what they're doing to the outside world, or even to their own employees. I suspect that this reticence is linked to a lot of reasons. First and foremost among them is being brought up Christian or Jewish, in both of which religions people were taught from an early age to help the sick and give to the poor, but never to let anyone know about it. The concept is that by talking about the good that you've done, you somehow sully it and make it objectionable. It is hard to get people—even fiercely competitive, smart corporate leaders—to get over this upbringing. But I would imagine that after the April 2008 riots in Haiti, Digicel is glad it has been telling its CSR story—and telling it often.

As soon as you communicate your CSR, you *will* be held up to a much higher standard and level of scrutiny. Expectations will rise. But as discussed in the introduction, expectations for companies to operate in society's best interests are at an all-time high, and perceptions that companies *are* operating in society's best interests are at an all-time low. The only way to narrow this gap, which has resulted in a lack of trust of business, is to tell your CSR story, your CSR reality.

You will quite possibly be criticized for your good works, but aren't there far worse things for which to be criticized? Most companies should be relieved if the only criticism they get is for trying to improve energy efficiency or for clearly labeling the carbon footprint of their products or for educating consumers on diamond mining in Africa.

McDonald's is one of the companies that have been extremely concerned about the risks in telling its CSR story. Why? Because it is afraid people are going to doubt what it says just because it is McDonald's. This company provides assistance to five thousand families of hospitalized children a week through its Ronald McDonald House Charities (RMHC). In addition to helping these seriously ill children and their families, RMHC extends its reach by helping other not-for-profit organizations that directly serve and enhance the lives of children worldwide. And RMHC has a network of local chapters in fifty-one countries and regions and has awarded hundreds of millions of dollars in grants and program services to improve the lives of many children. More people should know more about this story even if they have been blessed enough never to have had to use RMHC's services for an ill child.

My comment to McDonalds is, "I don't know how you could *not* brand that." Yes, people will criticize you, but you are the world's leading fast-food company. People already do criticize you and, as a leader, they always will. You've just got to get used to that idea and continue to emphasize the positive things you are doing in the community and for your customers. Although you can't fully control the risk you face, you can certainly help to shape the story and the debate about what you do and do not do.

Other Risks to Consider

There are other risks of telling your story than just the possibility that you will be criticized in the press or by NGOs or others for whom being cynical is easy. One such risk is the possibility your company will start down the CSR path, raising expectations of employees and other stakeholders, but then the mood or makeup of management or your board changes, and the CSR program is downgraded in importance or halted altogether. Unfortunately, we all know that business is fraught with management fads. A book comes out about some new way to motivate employees to remarkable new levels of effectiveness, calculate profits per employee, slice costs to the bone, and strike fear in the hearts of competitors. Or a superstar CEO experiences meteoric success, and everyone wants to know how he or she did it—and how they can do it too. Before you know it, the fad is in full swing, and everyone is doing it, at least until people get bored with it and the next fad comes along.

I have found that a CSR business strategy—if effectively linked to objectives and competencies and executed smartly—is difficult to reverse because it can add to your bottom line both directly and indirectly. It can also make people feel good about your company, become loyal to it, trust it, and be motivated to work for it. Often these trends don't let you reverse your company's CSR direction.

I believe that as problems in the world become more intractable, governments become weaker, and resources continue to shift to the private sector, CSR is here to stay. Surely for some companies CSR might just be the fad du jour. Doing a CSR program because it is trendy is unfortunate and is mainly for the companies that are not engaged in smart, effective, strategic CSR. Some business leaders may drop or at least scale back their CSR strategies once the mileage they get out of them with customers or other stakeholders diminishes or their budgets grow tighter. If they do, these companies will not only lose the very real benefits that a corporate social responsibility strategy can bring them, but they will dash raised employee expectations, most likely resulting in lowered engagement, productivity, and loyalty. And consumers will likely switch to the company's competitor that has been able to both develop an effective CSR strategy and tell its CSR story.

It's also highly risky to walk into a business school and give presentations telling students how important CSR is to your business, and how you want employees to be fully engaged in the process and to help guide it, and then do nothing of the sort when these students sign on as employees. Believe it or not, this kind of scenario happens all the time. Recent hires who finds themselves in the company that touted during recruitment an extreme commitment to CSR will not only soon be looking for a new job, but they will also be telling anyone who will listen that your company talks nonsense.

Another risk is that a company will miscalculate in its CSR message. Dove's Campaign for Real Beauty was discussed in chapter 3. Even a savvy brand like Dove can occasionally make a mistake. It's how a company recovers from mistakes that is the critical factor. When it first started advertising the real-woman campaign, Dove attached it to an anticellulite cream product, a campaign that obviously backfired. It seemed that Dove's brand people weren't connected to its CSR people. However, Dove recovered quickly from that misstep. The Dove Campaign for Real Beauty is based on many years of solid research across the globe on how women define beauty, and the company has the substance to back it up.

Avoiding Communication Traps

Companies run into problems when they try to communicate one message, and that message is misinterpreted or misconstrued or the meaning is reversed from what was intended. How do you keep from falling into such a trap? As discussed, make sure your CSR program is backed up with substance. Then be confident in what you do—go in knowing that there are risks, and communicate smartly.

Many times companies get scared of doing the easiest thing: just communicating transparently. The litigiousness of our society gets in the way of transparency, and often the legal department is the biggest barrier to CSR communications inside a company. Nike got caught in the trap of trying to communicate the details of its factory conditions to university athletic directors. First the company said it gave workers a forty-minute break, and then it said it gave workers an hour break. It got tripped up in the details, which in the end weren't all that important. A man named Kasky sued Nike over this, and during the nearly two years when the case was being heard and reheard, Nike went silent about its CSR program, as did a lot of companies, out of fear of the Kaskys of the world.

It's better to develop a simple, clear, and consistent message that gets across the main idea in terms that are not overly detailed or technical. Sometimes the less you say, the better. A good story isn't good because it is highly detailed. A good story is good because it is simple, consistent with the storyteller's values and image, and engaging. Most people don't have the time or the inclination to care about the small print. They want to see the big picture and a story with impact.

It's getting to the place where the less transparent you are, the more you're going to have consumer watchdog groups digging into your doings. The more transparent you are, the less reason there is for people to dig deeper to find out whether or not you've got something to hide. The assumption is if you're not being transparent, you're hiding something. And the more suspect you become, the more probable it is that you're going to get in trouble—that someone's going to dig up something. As you learn in Communication 101—particularly as it relates to crisis communications—tell the truth and tell it fast.

Summary

Here's the real truth about telling your CSR story: stories trump facts ten times out of ten. Not seven times out of ten, not nine times out of ten, but truly ten times out of ten. That is not to say that having facts, collecting data, measuring impact, and so forth are not important. You certainly do need the facts to back up your CSR story. But leave these reams of facts for your eighty-page CSR report. Leave them to your Web sites, all of which should have a CSR section, since this is where consumers go first today for CSR information on a company. People often forget that the power of stories is in the telling, not in the facts that back up the story. Try the 80/20 rule when you have the CSR substance and are creating your CSR story. Focus 80 percent on the storytelling itself, and 20 percent on the facts.

For the rest of the time, in your marketing and branding and advertising, in your recruiting, in your company leadership speeches, and in your in-store signage and package messaging, tell a clear, consistent, compelling, and concise CSR story. If you have the substance to back it up, your competition won't have time to catch up with you. You'll take the early lead. The CSR storytelling space is wide open today in many sectors of most industries for companies to claim first-mover advantage.

PART III

What to Do on Monday Morning

Now that you've seen how to put together a powerful CSR business strategy and put the power of branding to work, it's time to take action. In Part III, you will find specific advice for what you can do right now to put the principles of this book to work. You'll learn how to make a plan for branding your CSR, how to measure the results in the right way, and what CSR trends to look out for in the future.

10

MAKE A PLAN

> In the world we are now entering, it is not only the mindset of multinational businesses that needs to change, but the skill set of the people we employ. Corporate social responsibility—having a positive impact on society—is no longer an optional add-on. It is an integral part of business strategy and business practice.
>
> —Patrick Cescau, group president, Unilever

When you make a plan, you greatly increase the probability of actually getting something done.

Here is a story called the Baby Parable: One day, four women were walking along a river in the woods. Suddenly, they came to a clearing and saw an onslaught of babies drowning in the river. Of course, the women were immediately catapulted into action. However, each woman took a different approach to saving the babies.

The first woman jumped in the river and began plucking babies out one by one and throwing them to safety on the riverbank. She worked swiftly and tirelessly to save as many babies as she could, one at a time. The second woman also jumped into the water, but instead of throwing the babies to shore one at a time, she started to teach the babies to swim so they could save themselves. The third woman ran upstream to see who was throwing the babies into the water to their deaths, in order to determine the cause of the problem and advocate for change. Finally, the fourth woman, probably a university professor, ran back to her office and jumped on her computer to do some research and analysis: What were the stats? Were the babies being thrown in from the south shore or the north? Was it only this clearing where they were drowning, or were there others? What was the temperature and depth of the water? What did the big picture tell them about this problem, and how could they educate others as to how to solve it?

If you run a company and have been doing any sort of CSR work, or even if you are a living being and have been approached by any sort of charitable cause, parts of this story probably ring true or resonate with you, at least in terms of how we approach change, philanthropy, and social and environmental causes. The first thing I instruct companies to do during their CSR planning is to ask themselves and their leadership, which strategy is the company most interested in executing? Few companies say that they wish to set out to save one baby at a time. I am clear in not advocating that one strategy is in any way better than another. In fact, for a country like Haiti, we need to do all we can using all four strategies.

Next I ask a company to list its preferred strategy and then plot everything that it is currently doing and plot it on a four-by-four grid, as shown below. Usually, most of what the company has been doing is in a different quadrant from where it says it wants to operate. From that point, we can start to make a plan.

Save the babies, one at a time	Teach the babies to swim
• Charity work • Serve desperate needs	• Empowerment work • Teach skills • Help people overcome problem
Run upstream to stop whoever is throwing the babies in	Analyze why people throw babies in rivers
• Advocacy work • See cause of suffering and work to stop it	• Problem analysis • Big-picture view • Learn about problem and share knowledge

Business leaders are accustomed to making strategic plans for their core business processes; they make, refine, and execute plans of all kinds on a regular basis. They make plans for acquisitions, for recruitment and hiring, for marketing, for budgeting, and for much more. However, while these leaders know the importance of planning for their core business processes, they often neglect to plan when it comes to CSR. To them, CSR is not as important or as urgent as their core business areas, or they think of CSR as something soft and fuzzy and nice to do once all other plans are set in motion—and certainly not as something they can understand and quantify easily. But you've learned by now that CSR can be as hard and tangible as any other core business process, and it can be budgeted for, strategized for, planned for, and measured.

Besides helping to get something done, planning offers several other benefits, which are just as important for CSR-related initiatives as they are for core business processes:

1. Planning *guides the choices* and decisions made by your organization about CSR efforts. The sum total of these choices determines the future and fortunes of your CSR efforts.

2. Planning allows you to *be proactive* rather than giving in to the tyranny of *reacting* to the urgent. If you want to achieve a specific goal, you must have clear priorities so that your teams of people will act in ways that will help reach the chosen future and the desired outcomes rather than using their energy dealing with the crisis du jour.

3. Planning allows you to *make an impact, succeed, and lead,* rather than just getting along. Every year, CSR strategies, initiatives, and programs come and go, and the cynics are able to say, "See, I told you this would never work!" Creating a successful CSR strategy and program doesn't happen by chance—it's the result of planned decisions and actions.

Whether you're the CEO or the president, an executive or middle manager, as a leader of your organization, you set the tone and the example for others to follow. If you make setting a priority, others will follow. If you set clear-cut goals, priorities, and objectives, your employees will work toward them, your customers will notice your impact, and you will likely achieve positive results. If you can't seem to find the time to bother with the planning process—downgrading its importance in the eyes of those around you—then no one else will either.

A Step-by-Step Approach to Making a Plan

The flood of information, issues, opportunities, and problems with which you deal every day can threaten your ability to focus on the things that are most critical to the success of your business's CSR program. Unless you have a plan—with clearly assigned tasks, goals, and responsibilities— then even the best CSR program can go awry. So make a CSR plan first, then execute it, then measure it, and then tell your story.

My least favorite consulting task is when a company's executives hire me to develop its CSR strategic plan from my consulting office, without talking to anyone inside or outside the firm, as if in a vacuum, and then deliver it to them. I have been asked a few times to just "give us your off-the-shelf CSR plan," as if each business's challenges, issues of fit, business objectives, and competencies were the same. My favorite consulting task is when a company's executives ask me to come in and help them in developing their CSR strategy by engaging with the business, both inside and outside of the firm. They ask me to be the facilitator of their CSR plan making.

Here is my suggested approach to making a plan:

Step 1: Assign someone to be in charge—a CSR manager. You can't manage an effective CSR plan by committee. Ultimately, one person has to be in charge of the effort to ensure full accountability, efficiency, and communication, and to get people across the company engaged in developing strategy, creating champions, and encouraging ownership. Depending on the size of your organization, the job could be a part-time or a full-time one. It could be offered to a new hire or to an existing employee—ideally someone in your firm who has expressed deep interest in CSR, someone you want to engage and retain, and someone who already knows and understands your business and your operations. That is how it happened at eBay, where the senior manager of strategic growth and partnerships,

Gary Dillabough, found himself looking for a challenge after making the deals to bring Skype and PayPal to eBay. He went to Meg Whitman and told her that he wanted to quit. Whitman wisely wanted to keep him and was willing to do anything within reason to make that happen. He wanted to work on CSR, and Whitman was happy to comply.

Step 2: Conduct a CSR current assessment (internal). Look at all the things currently being done within your company's broad CSR endeavor, as well as things done in the past, and map them to your core business objectives and core competencies. Keep the ones that closely match up and are aligned, tweak the ones you can, and toss the rest. I am not telling you to immediately drop the commitment you made to the local home-less shelter in the middle of the year, leaving it unable to meet its budget and feed folks meals. Strategically and smartly phase out your misaligned partnerships and initiatives and clearly communicate that these endeav-ors fall outside of your new CSR strategy. Finally, look for gaps, missed opportunities, and vulnerabilities on which you can tack your strategic direction.

Step 3: Conduct a CSR competitive study of the CSR landscape (exter-nal). Look outside of your organization and identify the following:

- Issues for your industry
- Leaders, laggards, and the areas in which each operates
- Best practices, biggest failures, and overall learnings from those who traveled before you
- The sweet spot for you to enter, to make an impact, and to own

Step 4: Gather together a cross-functional CSR team within your com-pany. Pull the members from a variety of different functions and depart-ments and power areas in the firm, and choose CSR proponents as well as some of the more critical skeptics.

Step 5: Develop a CSR strategic plan. Let the cross-functional team from Step 4 brainstorm freely with no qualitative judgments as to the viabil-ity of their suggestions. This is my favorite part of the process, for when groups are turned loose through a creative process to develop a new strategy or direction on how the company can make money and improve the world, their hard work and outcomes are boundless. Your employees need to work this out together so there is ownership across the company. My favorite strategy is to assemble some employees into teams, give them the CSR strategy development assignment with clear-cut rules and parameters, give them a set time, and ask them to come back and report out to the large group in a competition, telling them that a winning team will be selected. You do not even have to have a prize: folks who work in corporations today tend to be competitive and driven and want to win. Encourage the emergence of champions and as much employee engagement as possible in the process of developing the strategic plan. Ask team members to take ownership over certain parts of the plan and to go back to their functional units and gain buy-in on the selected issue area that fits well with your company's mission, vision, and values, NGO partner(s), the elements of your strategy, a communication and branding plan, and metrics for success. Also be sure to set clear goals and agree on a realistic timeline.

Step 6: Sell the CSR strategic plan up, down, and throughout your company:

If you've done your job well up to this point, you have already developed a team of CSR strategy owners and hence believers to help sell your plan throughout the company. But don't forget to do the following:

- Get the people you need (CEO, CFO) to be not only on board but personally committed and engaged. Engaged means *involved,* not just saying "Yes, go do this."
- Build CSR messaging into existing internal channels, including CEO fireside chats, town halls, and all-hands meetings, recruiting, intranet, company newsletters, in-house messaging, performance appraisals, and displays in company facilities and offices (such as the company mission, vision, and values on display at Levi Strauss's front lobby at headquarters).
- Build CSR messaging into external communications, such as on your company's Web site, at the point of sale, in company reporting, in marketing and PR, and in NGOs' and other partners' messaging and communications.
- Begin to develop your CSR story components.

Step 7: Measure, report, communicate, and reevaluate your CSR strategy from time to time, just as you do with other core business strategies.

Step 8: Tell your CSR story consistently, in simple terms, and often.

Your Role as Leader

One of the things that makes planning particularly difficult for busy businesspeople is that you've got to set aside the time—often over several days, weeks, or months—to meet with your team to think about the present and the future. For leaders, especially the ones who are action oriented, it's easier (and often more exciting) to respond to pain, requests, and events than to try to anticipate them. Some people don't think they're doing their jobs unless they are dealing with and responding to several crises a day. They love the adrenaline rush that comes when they get to fight fires, think on their feet, juggle several things at once, and rally their employees to solve what could well be company-threatening problems.

The flood of information, issues, opportunities, and problems that you deal with every day can threaten your ability to do the things that are most critical to the success of your CSR strategy. If you're too busy worrying about detailed arrangements for the upcoming off-site directors' meeting, for example, you may miss the warning signs that a key CSR partner is getting some bad press for ethical violations and is about to drag your company down with it into a public and nasty mess.

As a leader, you might want to do everything, but the fact is that you *can't* do everything—at least not well. Because with CSR it could easily be argued that every cause is a good, worthy, and needed one, you want to address them all and micromanage them all, particularly due to the high risk associated with some of your CSR causes. But effective leaders learn that they have to separate what's important from what's not—keeping their focus where it most belongs, tracking the things that can make or break their CSR strategy, and leaving the rest to the other members of their teams.

As a CSR leader, manager, or champion, you need to delegate duties, responsibilities, and authority to others in your team. Here are a few reasons why:

- Your job is to concentrate your efforts on the things that you can do and your staff can't do.
- Delegation allows you to leverage your time and attention over a far greater number of employees and projects.
- Delegation gives you an opportunity to develop your employees' own skills, talents, and responsibilities.
- Delegation gets your employees more engaged in their jobs and the organization—leading to improved performance, increased loyalty, and heightened job satisfaction.
- Your success depends on it!

As a leader, you need to understand your business case for CSR, commit to it, take charge of the CSR planning process, make it a priority, involve others, provide the necessary resources, keep it on track, and ensure that the plan is adhered to once it is produced. In a small organization, you may do it all. In a larger organization, however, you'll need to rely on your team to provide vital input and support to the process, both before and after a CSR strategy is developed.

As leader of the planning effort, your specific roles are to do the following:

- Ensure that CSR planning is an ongoing process and an essential component of your organization. Establish a planning process with regular meetings and milestones. Hold people accountable for fulfilling their roles, such as participating in off-site meetings, completing work assignments between off-site meetings, communicating the finished plans to their departments, and fulfilling the charters of their teams.
- Let people know you expect their best thinking during the CSR planning process, and make sure to give your best yourself in planning meetings. Stretch your own and other people's thinking. Consider having planning meetings at an off-site location so they are not interrupted by phone calls, e-mail, routine problems, visitors, and other distractions.
- Keep people aligned with the plan, listen to suggestions and innovations, support continued discovery, and address people's

issues. Make a point of including employee suggestions and innovations in your plans whenever possible and then be sure they are acted on.

- Keep discovering new ideas and continuously fine-tuning the plan as outside forces change the environment in which you're working. Plans are living documents, and they should always reflect the most current realities of your business, the competition, and the competitive environment.

- Track progress and make regular reports to all employees about what's been achieved, how well the company is performing versus plan, what still needs to be accomplished, and how it needs to be accomplished within the culture of the company. Use the results to make adjustments to the plan and to drive your future planning efforts.

Mitigate Your Risk

In today's business world, the risks to a company for communicating its CSR work are high. A large oil company announces that it is cutting refinery hydrocarbon emissions by X percent over the next five years, and some environmentally active nonprofit pans the move as greenwashing (and, by the way, the company should make the cuts over three years, not five). Or a big-box retailer affiliates with a nonprofit organization and rolls out a multimillion-dollar advertising campaign that cobrands the partners' CSR initiative, only to have the relationship flame out when it is discovered that the nonprofit has been siphoning contributions into the director's personal bank account that has paid for a lavish lifestyle of private jets, expensive dinners, and Caribbean cruises.

Of course, today's bloodthirsty press colludes to make sure that every supposed transgression is noticed and is publicly discussed and dissected ad nauseum. I have tangled with many a journalist by asking the simple question of why the media refuse to cover the many good works that companies are doing in the world, in balance with the scandals. The person's response to me each time? If it bleeds, it leads; we serve the desires of our readers. There are also plenty of business-hating cynics who would love nothing more than to knock a good-professing company off its pedestal and prove that the company is—beneath its thin green skin—dishonest. Even the most idealistic and hopeful among us may find that we believe, on some level, that a company that espouses to be doing something good must be covering up for doing something bad. Or we immediately question the company's intentions for doing something good, despite the fact that its intentions—whatever they might be—do not change the very real and positive impact of its CSR on the world.

Is branding and communicating your CSR risky? Sure. But everything you do in business has an element of risk, and as with most things, the higher the risk, the higher the return.

A Step-by-Step Approach to Mitigating Your Risk

For a company about to invest millions of dollars in financial, human, and other resources in creating and executing its CSR strategy, the question of risk is quite real. But for the most part this risk can be anticipated, contained, and in some cases greatly mitigated. By taking the following steps before, during, and after you roll out your CSR program, you will be able to minimize the risk.

Step 1: Develop the substance of your corporate social responsibility first, create your CSR plan second, and communicate the plan and your results third. The easiest way to become a target of cynics and gadflies who might accuse your firm of greenwashing is to fail to first develop the substance of your company's CSR. Just applying a CSR label to your products doesn't make your company socially responsible, and people can easily see through such hollow attempts when they take a closer look at your company and what it does. Don't create your CSR plan until your company has the commitment to back it up, and don't communicate your results until you have a plan that effectively directs your company's CSR efforts.

Step 2: Stick with simple, consistent messaging. The best messages are simple, sweet, and easy to understand. Pages of facts and figures—no matter how truly wonderful they are—are going to get lost on the majority of consumers, and the facts and figures require a lot of time and money to produce. Consider the example of British grocer Tesco, which put a simple airplane symbol on packaging for its products that are air freighted into the country from elsewhere. In this case, a picture is worth a thousand words. The facts and figures belong in your CSR report, if you choose to do one, or on your Web site, or in your internal reporting that is used to develop and refine your CSR plan and strategy.

Step 3: Start small and focused—go for small wins and low-hanging fruit first so you can gain momentum from early successes. You can easily get caught in the trap of trying to make a BIG statement right out of the chute, hoping to attract lots of attention and publicity for your CSR effort. However, big statements take a lot of work and time to plan, execute, and measure, and there's no guarantee that you'll get the results you seek. It's fine to go for audacious goals. You can also set and execute a few smaller goals; involve and engage your employees, customers, and other stakeholders in achieving them; and then build on those successes as you work to attain your bigger goals over time. Small failures on the way to great successes are easier to tolerate within an organization than are large (public and expensive) failures. Programs that fail in a big way usually do not last long.

Step 4: Persevere in working your CSR strategy and plan. As we've discussed, you *will* be criticized—all good-doers are—but always keep in mind what you're being criticized for: trying to do good. If you keep plugging away at your strategy and plan, suffering the slings and arrows along the way that all leaders in this world take, you will certainly win the allegiance of your customers, the energy and motivation of your employees, and the approval of more than a few cynics and naysayers, too.

Step 5: Engage critics up front. Do not ignore your critics or try to throw them off your scent by issuing a flood of press releases or feel-good media pieces. They will not be so easily dissuaded, and if you anger them, they will make a sport of criticizing your CSR efforts, creating an even larger headache for you down the road. Instead, invite your critics into your process of developing your CSR strategy, metrics, and communication.

McDonald's is one of the companies that does this best, inviting its staunchest critics in to help find solutions and develop strategy. It is easy to sit back and criticize companies for their wrongdoing. It takes more intelligence to also recommend a set of viable solutions. The stakeholder teams advising companies like Dow Chemical, Wal-Mart, and McDonald's on their CSR strategy are made up of individuals from environmental and labor NGOs, university professors, and researchers on socially responsible investment. Several of the members of these teams began as critics of the companies and their procedures. If you can get your critics on your side and get their help in developing your plans, they will be much less likely to criticize you when you execute your plans.

Step 6: Engage your friends and "family" too. The most credible voices to communicate your CSR efforts are your nonprofit partners and the people who benefit, both directly and indirectly, from your good works. Your employees can also serve as voices of support for your CSR effort, as they are on the front lines of your business every day and are more believable than your corporate communications department. Ask your NGO partners and recipients of your good works in the community to communicate your progress as you execute your CSR strategy and plan. Find as many ways as possible for them to communicate—through community meetings, press releases, interviews in newspapers and television and other media, blogs, and their own Web sites. The more varied the sources of the good news about your CSR efforts—in terms of sources and geographic and socioeconomic distribution—the better.

Step 7: Be proactive in communicating your CSR, not reactive in responding to someone else's criticism. When it comes to getting the word out about your corporate social responsibility efforts, once you have your CSR strategy in place and are working your plan, you can, and should, start talking about your successes—and even your failures—along the way to your ultimate goals. Several years ago, Wal-Mart set the almost impossible sustainability goal of zero waste. Instead of waiting to achieve this goal, which may be many years in coming, it communicated early and often on its progress, even admitting that it had made some missteps on the road to its ultimate destination. This transparency has helped build credibility for Wal-Mart's sustainability efforts in the face of a vocal army of critics who are suspicious of just about anything the company does.

It's Not a Question of If;
It's a Question of When—and How

Anytime you announce that you've experienced a CSR success or achieved one of your goals or entered into a partnership with a nonprofit organization that's prominent in the area of your chosen interest, the cynics will be unremitting in their efforts to prove that your intentions are less than noble. Communicating your CSR work does open up your organization to public examination and risk, and you *will* be held up to a high standard.

But the outcomes can actually be positive ones for your organization. The result might be that you'll be seen by the public as more worthy of trust, loyalty, patronage, and investment. Wal-Mart has gotten much bad press over the years for supposedly destroying the fabric of American small business. However—surprise, surprise—its CSR strategy is beginning to bear fruit as increasing numbers of people begin to realize that Wal-Mart really means to do what it says. Its actions are speaking loudly—far more loudly than words ever could.

The question is not *whether* to communicate your CSR. The question is *how best to do it*. Working with your nonprofit partners on your communication strategy, for example, can be a successful path to developing your communication strategy. By their nature nonprofits are far more trusted than are corporations. This perception makes sense since nonprofits have a social mission, while corporations exist primarily to make a profit for their shareholders.

So let your nonprofit partners do the talking about your CSR partnerships and the impact on their own missions, and on the communities and people they serve. Offer your partners the communications, branding, and advertising resources that your marketing department surely has. They will likely jump at the opportunity, as most nonprofits are horribly understaffed and under-resourced—particularly in the marketing and communications functions. Put the objectives and goals of the nonprofit on the table together with your own. Develop your message authentically, together. And together cobrand your work.

You *will* be criticized. But it seems to me that there are far worse things for which to be criticized than trying to do good in this world, for having and branding hope that is backed by authenticity, substance, and strategic management. The real risk is that as soon as a company tries to communicate its good works, it will be held to a higher standard. While this can surely *feel* risky, it is indeed the only way you can stretch and continue to be all you can be—and serve all those you can serve—in this world. We all need to be held to the highest standards of conduct to continually improve and grow.

At the end of the day, remember: you cannot not communicate. By not communicating anything that you are doing in the area of CSR, you are, in fact, communicating something.

Increasing the Probability of Success

While making a plan won't guarantee that your CSR strategy will happen, or that it will turn out well, making a plan will certainly increase the probability that you will succeed on both counts. The more effort you and your team put into the planning process, the more engaged your team will be and the better prepared everyone will be to fulfill their roles in your company's CSR process when the time comes. Of course, there are risks in rolling out your CSR strategy—nothing in business has zero risk. Take time to consider ways to mitigate your risk and to ensure that your CSR experience is a good one.

11

MEASURE SMART

In God we trust; all others bring data.
—W. Edwards Deming

As with all things in business, the adage "what gets measured gets done" holds true for corporate responsibility, too. Beyond simply getting done, the things that get measured get evaluated, reassessed, retooled, and done better. And the things that get done better do not get cut from the budget in an economic downturn or a slow quarter. Hence, the problem with the old form of corporate responsibility—philanthropy—is that philanthropic budgets tended to be tied to profitability and sales, and when those sales went down, so too did the levels of philanthropic giving.

As we have seen, a CSR business strategy can and should be part of your core business operations. It can be a competitive advantage for your firm and, if done strategically and effectively, should contribute to your overall profitability. In this chapter, we'll consider how best to measure your CSR, the different kinds of measures to consider, and what to do with all that data once you've got it.

Smart Measuring: A Suggested Approach

CSR advocates and managers generally try to measure anything and everything in an effort to prove its worth. They measure everything that can be measured and end up not measuring anything consistently or well. Measurement is difficult, and this problem is not unique to CSR. Measuring things such as the value of innovation, brand, advertising returns to share price, and the impact of research and development are difficult, too. That does not mean companies don't value it or do it.

Here is my suggested approach to measuring smartly—and bringing value to your CSR efforts in the process.

Start by selecting metrics that are directly linked to your core business objectives. Every company has core business objectives. For example, Hewlett-Packard's core business objectives are growth, efficiency, and access to capital. So when it sets out to measure progress on its chosen CSR strategies, it should start by measuring, for example, the impact of these initiatives on HP's growth: did the company's energy optimization strategy penetrate new markets or new customer segments or win big government contracts? Start first by showing what your CSR strategy did to support your overall corporate strategy.

Select CSR metrics linked to your stated CSR focus areas. In the case of Wal-Mart, the focus areas are waste, energy, and sustainability. So Wal-Mart should be looking at developing two or three good metrics in each of these areas. For Pedigree, the focus is pet adoption, which makes for clean and simple measurement: how many pets have been adopted into loving homes, and how much money has Pedigree given to dog shelters so that they could support pet adoption?

Start by picking a few things to measure, three to five at most, and measure them well. Get some results and determine if your measurements are accurate, if they are valid, if you can see positive change and impact over time, and if your CSR strategy is working, and communicate this. Then add a few more metrics. Don't do what most companies do and try to measure everything that can be measured from the start. Your CSR strategy will probably be killed by some smart CFO who is not seeing the impact because while you are busy trying to measure a hundred different things, none of them are related to the business goals that your CFO has been charged with tracking. I have seen countless companies in which a story around one or two solid metrics from a CSR strategy has saved its life, and I have seen countless other companies whose CSR—even the best-laid intentions and well-developed strategies—has been cut while the CSR team was working hard to execute on a metrics plan that looked more complex than an explanation of the Bosnian war.

Pick a few key *input* metrics (such as money given or employees' time volunteered) and a few *impact* metrics (such as homelessness eliminated or increases in self-esteem). Most companies seem to be unduly fond of the input side of the metrics equation. They produce page after page in their CSR reports that track thousands of employees' volunteer hours in a hundred different countries working with three hundred different causes. They speak about the thousands of dollars given to two hundred nonprofits, each representing a different societal or environmental issue. They expound on the millions of bars of soap shipped to the New Orleans area after Hurricane Katrina hit. But these companies fail to communicate the impact: What was the *impact* of the hours their employees worked in the community? How many new houses were built in South Central Los Angeles, taking how many people off the streets or out of homeless shelters, and giving how many kids access to a steady elementary school education that they did not previously have? Those are the significant impacts of these employees' valuable time, and they make for a great CSR story. I suspect that companies typically focus more on input than impact for two reasons. First, it's simply easier to count hours and dollars and bars of soap. Second, most companies' CSR strategies are spread so thinly across so many different unrelated causes and issues that they have been unable to make a big impact in any one area. Whirlpool is lucky because it has to measure the inputs and impacts on only one area: homelessness. Actually, Whirlpool is not just lucky; it is smart.

Pick a few *company-impact* metrics (such as increases in sales or number of new markets entered) and a few *social or environmental* metrics (such as fewer plastic bags used or the decrease in energy used). Here is a tricky balance for CSR leaders inside of companies trying to prove their worth and maintain their jobs. They need to show that their work has positive impact on the company in terms of increased sales, savings from higher energy efficiency, or reduced turnover because of increased employee satisfaction. That part makes sense and is critically necessary.

But if the carefully developed CSR strategy is not having a positive impact on the environment or society, then it is not truly CSR and is just another good sales strategy or human resources initiative and should be labeled as such. Recall that my definition for CSR is that it has to be of positive value to the company as well as to the environment or society. So don't forget to track and measure your CSR strategy's impact on the world outside your company, or the critics will go after you.

Of the three or four key metrics selected, think of a few ways to articulate the value of each.

- Monetary value (the dollar value of those 300,000 employee volunteer hours or 600,000 bars of soap donated)
- Financial value
- Quantitative value
- Qualitative value
- Story or narrative

In other words, the game is not to have more metrics but to measure the same thing and articulate its value in five different ways, or at least three of these five different ways. This is a hard one for companies whose employees have been trained to articulate all value in only one way: money. Consider, after you have calculated the financial value, how else you can articulate the value of building of eighty homes in South Central Los Angeles. And remember, stories trump facts. That is not to say that you should forget the facts, but you should develop and communicate the story and use the facts to back up the story. One good story about a family who is now living in a home built by Habitat for Humanity and Whirlpool employees and outfitted with Whirlpool Energy Star energy-efficient appliances can go a long way. It has value, stickiness, and impact, even for a company that makes large, heavy, cold metal objects.

Talk about the positive and the negative measurements. If your CSR plan is producing positive metrics, congratulations! Talk about how well it's doing. If your CSR plan is *not* producing positive metrics, talk about that openly and honestly and about what your plan is to change that outcome. Openness is disarming, a rarely used corporate strategy. You will gain huge first-mover advantages by being open—take advantage of them! It is highly improbable that you will get it right the first time and have positive numbers on all of your CSR metrics. CSR is a complex strategy.

Review your metrics and adjust. Take a look at your metrics from time to time to be sure that you're getting the results you expect. If not, find other metrics that get you the data you need. Or go back and tweak your CSR strategy, improve it, refine it, and execute it more smartly.

Now that you've seen what the key steps are for smart measuring, let's take a look at some of these steps in more detail, and consider some real-world examples of who's doing it right—and who's doing it not quite right.

Measure What Matters to Your Core Business Objectives

When it comes to measuring their CSR, many companies aren't very smart about it. Instead of focusing on just a few things to measure, they try to measure everything. And instead of looking at the big picture, they get buried in the details of pages of numbers and graphs and charts that few consumers will understand, much less bother to look at or try to understand. If I have one essential recommendation when it comes to measuring your CSR, it is to measure only a few things and measure them well instead of measuring many things poorly.

Start with what matters to the company; what is valued in the overall corporate strategy. Take, for example, the corporate strategy for Hewlett-Packard that we discussed in chapter 1.

Three things matter most to HP's senior management: growth, efficiency, and access to capital. If HP's CSR strategy was developed effectively, the pillars of its CSR strategy would be somehow linked to one or all of these three business objectives.

For example, reducing energy use throughout the company is clearly linked to HP's efficiency and capital strategies, so the CSR department would be wise to pick one to three metrics related to efficiency, such as recapturing and reusing wastewater or waste from its master grinder (which grinds up used product) and one to three metrics related to capital savings, metrics such as realizing savings from reductions in energy use. In developing its e-inclusion initiative (now defunct), which brought technology to developing world countries such as India and Pakistan, the CSR department would select a metric related to access to new and growing markets.

In addition to developing a few effective metrics related to the business objectives of the firm, companies should also pick a few metrics focused on measuring value to society. Measuring value to the firm is critical to sustaining the CSR strategy in the company's overall strategy portfolio, but ultimately if the company is adding no value to society or to the environment, then the sustainability of the strategy is a moot point. If it is only creating value for the firm and not to society or the environment, then it is not corporate social responsibility at all.

Measure Your Stated CSR Focus Areas

We can use the HP example to illustrate the measurement of CSR focus areas. As it turns out, a cross-functional team of HP employees did set the company's CSR focus areas through a strategic process starting with the core corporate strategy. In 2006, HP decided on the following priorities for its CSR strategy:

- **Energy.** Improving energy efficiency and innovation in HP's operations and products.

- **Product take-back and recycling.** Reducing product environmental impacts through leading-edge reuse and recycling solutions.

- **Responsible supply chain.** Raising standards in HP's global supply chain and ensuring responsible manufacturing for all products.

- **Education.**

When deciding what to measure and how, most firms start with the things that are easy, as opposed to the things that make up their stated CSR priorities. Assuming that HP decides to do the latter rather than the former, here's the course of action it should take:

First, it must develop a layer of metrics around the company's overall stated corporate strategy objectives, defining one to three strong metrics around each corporate objective.

Next, it should look to its stated CSR focus areas and develop one to three strong metrics for each. For example, for the energy focus area, HP could measure its increase in the number of Energy Star–certified products, meaning that its products would become increasingly energy efficient. It could measure its own reduction of energy use through its LEED-certified (Leadership in Energy and Environmental Design–certified) building program for its own real estate. It could measure its reduction of water use at corporate headquarters or its reduction of server storage energy use through its smart-cooling networking centers, which capture outdoor air in the colder months for network-cooling processes.

I recommend that HP have one to three metrics per focus area and measure consistently. The metrics should be consistent so they show change over time, as opposed to measuring, say, twenty different areas and changing those year to year. When evaluating a company's CSR report the question to ask is, *how do these numbers relate to last year or the year before?* For the most part, companies want to show measurement changes over time, so they need to stick with the same set of metrics, even if they expect little impact over time. Rather than changing metrics depending on what their critics are saying about them or what they feel they can measure, companies should stick to a consistent metrics regime over a period of time.

Fewer Metrics, Multiple Ways of Communicating Value

You are better off measuring a few things more thoroughly than measuring many things carelessly. The place to concentrate your efforts is not so much in *what* you measure but in *how you communicate* what you measure.

As you consider how you will go about communicating value, keep in mind that stories trump facts. I am not advocating abandoning the facts. Facts are critical, particularly internally when deciding what is working, what is not, what to cut, and what to fight for in budget season. And communicating measurements of your CSR impact can develop trust and credibility, among the socially responsible investment advisers, whose job it is to consider and pore over the facts.

For example, Denis O'Brien of Digicel had multiple ways of communicating his CSR program for one important prospective client. He launched the Digicel Foundation in 2004 to build communities and community spirit in the areas in which the company operates. The foundation's first undertaking was in Jamaica, where it built schools, launched and supported soccer teams, and supported post-hurricane rebuilding efforts. He got a rare opportunity to enter the Nicaraguan market when one day, out of the blue, he received a phone call telling him that he would have ten minutes to make a sales pitch—along with other telecommunications companies—to Nicaraguan president Daniel Ortega.

After many long hours of preparation and research, O'Brien entered the meeting ready with facts and figures about the competitive advantages his company could offer. And just in case he needed a bit of extra ammunition, he came prepared with the story of his mother, who had once taken part in a pro-Ortega demonstration, despite Ortega's somewhat authoritarian leadership of the country. However, before he had a chance to complete the story of his mother's rallies in support of the president or launch into the value of the Digicel telecom network, Mr. Ortega interrupted and said, "Listen, I know what you have done for the people and the communities of Jamaica and Haiti. We would be honored to have your company serve not only our mobile telecommunications needs but also the needs of our communities." A corporate CEO cannot get a better market entrance strategy than that!

Measure What Matters

We in the CSR community are making a mistake in assuming that the measurement of corporate social responsibility has to be an exact science. Take another hot topic in business today: innovation. Innovation is big in the corporate world right now, but I hear no one complaining that innovation is next to impossible to measure (which is indeed the case). But when it comes to CSR, everyone wants to know the exact measurements—how big, how many, how often, how many years, how much impact, how many species, how many tons of this, and how many kilograms of that. And they want the definitive study proving causality. Causality is nearly impossible to prove for many things that a business does routinely, things like advertising, training and development, and branding. The best you can do with these business strategies, just as with CSR, is to show a correlation with business success.

Of course, we do need *some* metrics, so the first thing I do is to divide them into two sets—measurement of impact to society and measurement of impact to the company.

If a company isn't having a positive impact on society—pet adoption, for example, in the case of Pedigree's Adoption Drive—with its chosen strategy, then it's not the right strategy. And the cynics are going to try to prove that your strategy has no impact on society. However, if you can point to your metrics—"here's how many dollars we've contributed to the American Humane Association (AHA), and here's how many cities are active in our program, and here's the amount by which pet adoption rates have increased"—then you'll be able to counter the naysayers.

Although external metrics are important, internal metrics linking to business strategies and goals may be even more important. For example, if Pedigree's brand managers can point to their adoption program and say, "We were able to steal market share from Iams because of this campaign," then there's a good chance Pedigree will continue with the program, and perhaps even expand it. They can't prove causality, because many things can drive increases in sales, but they can show a correlation between the adoption program and the increase in sales. If you want your CSR to be a sustainable business strategy, you have to link it to a selected number of metrics inside your company.

Attach your CSR strategy to metrics that matter within your corporate culture. Every corporate culture has things that matter. Most corporations are going to have a culture that says that sales increases matter and that stealing market share from your competitors matters. So if you can, link the metric to some sort of an increase in sales or consumer loyalty. And don't forget internal metrics, such as employee satisfaction or engagement, which are important, too.

The Struggle to Connect Core Business and CSR Metrics

Many companies struggle to find the right metrics for their CSR efforts—and then to link them with the metrics that they routinely produce for their core business functions. Oil companies, for example, are in the business of drilling holes in the ground, extracting oil, and sending that oil to refineries, which then create a variety of petroleum-based products, including gasoline, diesel fuel, plastics, fertilizer, and asphalt. Sometimes these oil companies sell directly to consumers through company-owned gas stations, and sometimes they don't, instead selling their products to other businesses that handle the refining and retailing end of things. Consider the following corporate mission of an oil company: "To drill and extract oil in a way that leaves the communities we enter with a dignified, improved quality of life."

The drilling and extracting oil numbers can be measured easily. "The company drilled three hundred new oil wells in the previous fiscal year, and extracted 3 billion barrels of oil worldwide." However, the numbers for a dignified and improved quality of life are not so simple. Measuring things like quality of life or dignity is hard. Not only that, but these are not exactly the kind of things most companies are used to paying attention to, let alone measuring.

Most companies measure all the time—it's standard operating procedure. Royal Dutch Shell knows how many barrels of oil it pumped last week, Wal-Mart knows how many screwdrivers it sold yesterday, and Amazon knows how many copies of any book sold in the past hour. But, perhaps understandably, these same companies often face an ongoing challenge in measuring their CSR programs and then communicating the results in a way that is readily understandable by consumers.

Tell Stories with Your Metrics

If Wal-Mart says it has three key objectives in the CSR world—create zero waste, use 100 percent renewable energy, and sell sustainable products—then having just one to three metrics for each of these three objectives is enough. Wal-Mart doesn't need to have seven different metrics for each of these three objectives because it quickly gets too complex. Minimize the number of metrics, and be sure that each metric is one around which you can tell a story or provide an image or symbol.

I tell companies to pick just one to three metrics and tell a story or create an image or symbol for each in ten different ways. What sticks in consumers' minds when they're in the store buying Pedigree dog food is not the number of dogs that were saved from the gas chamber last year. It's the image from the Pedigree commercial of Echo, the dog with the woeful expression as he's sitting in the cage. That's what people remember.

So embellish your metrics with a story or image or symbol. This doesn't mean you don't need the numbers to back up your story or image. You do, but you also need to provide consumers with information they can understand and easily use and apply in their lives. For example, as discussed in chapter 8, Tesco uses an airplane symbol, which tells consumers that a product is air freighted into the United Kingdom from another country. You look at it on the package, and you immediately understand. You don't have to understand the numbers—the number of tons of CO_2 that an aircraft released into the atmosphere as it was flying your asparagus into the country from Peru. You just see the symbol, and you understand it.

Addressing the Fear of Going Public with Metrics

Credibility and trust are important things for any company to earn and maintain with its many stakeholders, from employees to customers to vendors and shareholders and others with whom the company does business. Most business leaders know that credibility and trust are important, yet they are fearful of going public with their CSR metrics. "What if the results are negative? Will that make us look as though we've failed?" "What will the cynics say if we don't achieve our CSR goals, but our sales are going up?" "What if the press gets wind of this?" Actually, questions like these make it particularly important for companies to communicate *all* of their CSR metrics—even if they turn out to be negative. There are a couple of good reasons for doing this.

First, when you are willing to communicate the good news—and the bad—you show that you deserve the trust you have earned in the marketplace and with your stakeholders. Your credibility can only go up.

Second, if you're getting negative results, you can reevaluate and your strategy and improve it, and then you can roll out the new strategy to the public so people can see that you aren't content to just rest on your laurels. Negative results are really not a bad thing—you learn from negative data. Not only that, but when you figure out how to solve your problems and your metrics eventually go positive, the impact will be more dramatic.

It's true that there is a lot of cynicism about CSR strategies, and it is not just on the part of the usual NGOs and corporate gadflies. Cynicism often rears its head among a company's employees, its shareholders, and other stakeholders. Some employees take a look at the latest socially oriented company initiative, and they think to themselves that it's just a CEO's pet project, or that it's simply the cause of this month and will soon be something different.

Unfortunately, some companies have been less than sincere in their CSR efforts, and employees and stakeholders have on occasion had good reason to wonder if the latest CSR campaign isn't just more of the same. But when companies finally decide to get serious and can say, "No, we're doing this because it is actually contributing to our growth," employees understand that and feel good about that because it makes their jobs more secure. Even if employees have nothing to do with their company's CSR, they feel not only proud about working for a company that is making a positive contribution to society but proud that their company is still keeping on track when it comes to meeting its business objectives.

One of Hewlett-Packard's business objectives is grabbing market share away from Apple and Dell. If you can show that these CSR campaigns are helping increase market share in India at Dell's expense, then you know you're doing something that matters to the company. As we saw in chapter 6, for Meg Whitman of eBay it was all about growth. So the eBay CSR champions were smart. They knew that what mattered to Whitman was growth, but they also knew that the company had an internal business challenge related to employee recruiting and retention. So they launched a global citizenship innovation competition internally, and they showed how many employees entered, participated, and got engaged in it. They compared these numbers with those from the last employee cause du jour. The results? Eight times as many employees got involved, and the effort resulted in the launch of a new market poised for growth: the market for fair-wage art from all around the world (eBay's purchase of World of Good was discussed in chapter 3). That can lead to growth!

Hewlett-Packard's E-inclusion Initiative

Let's dig a little deeper into Hewlett-Packard's e-inclusion initiative and see how the lack of meaningful metrics caused its untimely demise. The story begins in 2000 when HP decided to make a concerted effort to transfer technology across the digital divide by bringing HP technology to parts of the world that didn't have it. Unfortunately, the story ended just five years later, in 2005, when the program was cut after Carly Fiorina left and was replaced as CEO by Mark Hurd. Although no small part of the program's demise was a direct result of an aggressive focus on cost cutting on the part of HP's new management, I believe that another important reason was that the e-inclusion team at HP didn't have metrics that tied the program's social mission to its business mission.

In just one example, e-inclusion could have showed—but didn't—how its initiatives in India were not only helping poor people in that country but were also training a future workforce that the company needs because it is outsourcing a good deal of its work to India. E-inclusion didn't need a large number of metrics. It just needed one to three that were linked to what the company cared about, which was growth and market share. One such metric could have focused on the training and development of a future workforce in India. Another metric could have focused on securing a major Indian government contract with the technology.

Absent any such metrics, Mark Hurd could easily decide to cut the e-inclusion program—he just didn't see its business relevance. The lack of metrics wasn't the only reason that it got cut, but cutting the program was one of the first things that Mark Hurd did when he took the CEO position. HP was facing some major financial challenges as a company, and he needed to turn the numbers around quickly and show results to

HP's shareholders. With no obvious connection to the company's business results, e-inclusion had a big bull's-eye painted on it.

So anytime you're developing a new strategy around CSR, first be sure to determine your key performance indicators and metrics up front. Next, be sure to have metrics related both to the impact on society as well as the impact on the company.

Conclusion

CSR, TOMORROW AND BEYOND

It is never too late to be what you might have been.
—Maria Craik, *A Life for a Life*

To this point, we have discussed how to create a top-notch CSR strategy and how to brand and communicate your CSR strategy for maximum impact. In this chapter, we will take a couple of steps back, and then take a look forward, to the future of CSR and the future of organizations and what you should start thinking about soon.

Companies in all industries are undeniably moving toward corporate social responsibility. If your company doesn't yet have a CSR strategy, then it probably will before long. Although many reasons may account for this shift in corporate attitudes, the most insistent pressure for it is coming from consumers and prospective employees.

Three clear areas of business value for CSR are brand leverage, attraction of talent (aka human resources), and direct communication with consumers. Here are some facts from a survey on brands:

- Percentage who said they consider corporate citizenship when buying a company's product: 79
- Percentage who said that social responsibility is a big influence in their impressions of companies: 49
- Percentage who said that they would boycott a product if they learned about negative citizenship practices: 76
- Percentage who said they consider social commitment when choosing an employer: 77[44]

Despite consumers' interest in CSR, price and quality are still the most important factors for consumers. CSR may be a factor, but most buying decisions are still made on the basis of obtaining the best quality for the least amount of money, though for certain categories such as food, consumers have shown a willingness to pay about 15 percent more. Many consumers have a "what's in it for me?" attitude. With food, they see an advantage in putting the best antibiotic- and hormone-free, locally grown food in their kids' stomachs as well as their own. But I still typically advise companies never to lead with their corporate citizenship. Corporate citizenship should instead be linked in some way to the attributes of price or quality or both. Hormone-free means higher-quality chicken. Compact fluorescent light bulbs mean lower power-company bills.

General Electric does a great job of this type of linking with its Ecomagination program. The company links Ecomagination products not so much to price but to their potential to save customers money in operating costs. Let's say you're an executive for a railroad and you're in the market for a locomotive. According to Ecomagination Web site, by purchasing one of GE's new Evolution locomotives, you'll use 189,000 fewer gallons of fuel over the lifetime of the engine. With diesel fuel prices well over $4 a gallon in mid-2008, that's a savings of about $750,000. And, by the way, that same Evolution locomotive happens to be relatively green, producing 83 percent less particulates and 60 percent less nitrogen oxide emissions compared to GE locomotives produced twenty years ago. The Web site goes on to claim that "if every freight train in North America were pulled by an Evolution Series locomotive, the annual reduction in nitrogen oxide emissions would be equivalent to removing 48 million cars from the road each year."

This kind of information makes sense to buyers of locomotives, and to consumers, as it speaks both to the impact to them (their budgets) and the impact on the environment (lower emissions).

Global Corporate Social Responsibility Trends

Whether or not you support doing something about global warming, trying to feed the world, or finding a cure for AIDS, breast cancer, or autism, companies in increasing numbers are becoming involved in these and many other social and environmental issues. But rather than following the old-style model of philanthropy, which required them to just write out a big check every year, companies are involving their employees, their business partners, and other stakeholders in bringing about change themselves.

If you are serious about helping to drive this change through your own company's CSR strategy, then you should be acutely aware of where global corporate social responsibility is headed in the future. CSR trend analysis done by experts in the field suggests the following:

- Consumers are increasingly interested in *taking action* on issues such as climate change.
- CSR and branding campaigns that resonate with consumers are those that address *consumers' interest,* provide *easy-to-digest information,* and spark *dialogue and action.*
- Reputable campaigns are those that are *innovative* and are substantiated by the company's *authentic* commitment and ability to demonstrate *tangible results* toward its CSR goals.
- *Partnerships,* either between companies or with NGO partners, will continue to be beneficial. They help build credibility, and they make sense, because no one company can go it alone against an issue as large as global warming or AIDS.
- The environment is going to continue to be a big focus for CSR programs, with a particular focus on sustainability and energy use.
- Consumers are increasingly looking for and buying recycled and locally produced products.
- CSR is not going away anytime soon. The Millennial generation, which is now in the workforce, is demanding these types of products and workplaces.
- Your competitors are developing CSR strategies. Don't let them get ahead of you, because it is difficult to catch up once you get behind. But be aware that CSR efforts do not tend to show quick results. CSR is a long-term venture.
- Foreign governments—including those of Brazil, India, and China—are starting to mandate CSR as a requirement for doing

business in their countries. Increasingly, having a viable and active CSR strategy will be a cost of entry for businesses in their international dealings.

- Look to BRIC countries (Brazil, Russia, India, and China) for sourcing, as companies have moved their supply chains and services there and will continue to do so. Consumer income is also mushrooming in these markets, so be sure to link your CSR efforts to your BRIC expansion plans.

In the future, the focus will be not on whether to engage in CSR but *how* to do it smarter, more strategically, and more integrally as part of companies' day-to-day business strategies. The focus will also be on how best to communicate and *brand* your CSR. Although still relatively young, the CSR space is getting crowded. However, the space of smart, effective, strategic CSR is less crowded, and the space of well-branded, well-communicated CSR is *wide open*, so grab the leadership spot in your industry now! And remember: CSR brands doing good, which increases hope. And if there's one thing we can all agree on, it's that the world could use more hope for a better future.

Changing Trust

There is a wide divergence between levels of trust in brands in the United States versus Europe. Although trust in nonprofits is generally high, Europeans put far more trust in certain nonprofits than do Americans. For example, 76 percent of Europeans trust the Amnesty International nonprofit brand versus only 40 percent of Americans, and 62 percent of Europeans trust the Greenpeace brand versus just 38 percent of Americans. Interestingly, this perception flips when people are asked about their trust in a selection of well-known corporate brands. While 56 percent of Americans trust the Coca-Cola brand, only 35 percent of Europeans do, and while 55 percent of Americans trust the McDonald's brand, only 26 percent of Europeans do.[45]

These perceptions are a problem for American companies that hope to expand their reach internationally. Companies are lacking in trust. They're also lacking in knowledge of the social and environmental issues

"What would you suggest to fill the dark, empty spaces in my soul?"

are coming their way. If McDonald's hadn't been lacking in knowledge of social issues, it would have seen the issue of widespread obesity coming its way. Today McDonald's is doing a far better job at future issues monitoring. If Ford and GM had had a better handle on environmental issues coming at them, they would be offering more and better fuel-efficient cars rather than fuel-hogging SUVs and pickup trucks.

What Companies Need (and What Nonprofits Have)

Companies tend to lack credibility when they communicate. They often forget to engage employees in their CSR opportunities. They lack the ability to differentiate their brands—particularly in highly commoditized market segments. And they lack a track record of doing good in the community.

By contrast, nonprofits have exactly what companies need. They are trusted. They understand social and environmental issues because they tend to be focused on the issues and on their mission. They are credible when communicating with the public because they're trusted. And they have fantastic opportunities to engage corporate volunteers.

Companies need

- Trust
- Knowledge of social issues
- Credible channels of communication
- Opportunities for employee engagement and volunteerism
- Differentiation of their brands
- Proven record of positively contributing to community

Nonprofits have

- Trust
- Knowledge of social issues
- Credible channels of communication
- Opportunities for employee engagement and volunteerism
- Differentiation of their brands
- Proven record of positively contributing to community

It seems like the perfect match. Of course, nonprofits need something too, but unfortunately they usually ask for the wrong thing. Typically non-profits just ask for money instead of telling companies that they can offer them all of the above and more. Nonprofit organizations that focus only on seeking financial donations are missing an opportunity.

A woman who ran a youth-focused antiviolence nonprofit organiza-tion in Dublin told me a story of how her organization was meeting with Intel in Dublin about working together on a youth-oriented program. During the course of the presentation to Intel, the parties decided to take a fifteen-minute break. The director of the nonprofit went outside to have a cigarette, and there was an Intel employee—a member of the Millennial generation—outside having a cigarette too. They introduced themselves, and the Intel employee asked her what she was doing at the company's facility. She told him that she was presenting some opportunities for Intel to get involved in antiviolence programs that her nonprofit ran for youth and women. The Intel employee perked up and said, "I really hope we work with you because I hate my job here, and that would make it so much better." At least one employee felt that the partnership with a nonprofit would increase his engagement with the company, and we all know that disgruntled employees tend to talk to other employees and "share their love," or lack thereof.

Nonprofits offer significant opportunities to companies because of the impact they have on communities. They can provide your employees with a sense that they are doing something important—something that will have a positive impact on their communities. And they can provide your employees with a way to take action by volunteering. But instead of showing companies all the things they can offer to them they typically just ask for money. This is a major missed opportunity for nonprofits.

One strategic partnership is between apparel maker Timberland and the nonprofit City Year. Timberland has been run by the Swartz family since Nathan Swartz became sole owner of the Abington Shoe Company in 1955 (the company officially changed its name to the Timberland Company in 1978). Nathan focused the company on producing footwear, and Timberland grew, largely on the sales of its famed leather Timberland hiking boot. When Nathan's son Sidney took over in 1986, he began a transition within Timberland, turning it into a brand company with the addition in 1988 of men's and women's apparel and the opening of Timberland specialty stores in Boston, New York, and London.

In 1989 the company created its first partnership with a nonprofit, City Year, and donated fifty pairs of boots for the organization's volunteer workers. This partnership grew, and the level of support reached more than $10 million from Timberland, enabling City Year to expand to eighteen cities. After Sidney's son Jeffrey took the position of COO in 1991 (he became president and CEO in 1998), the company began another transition, this time from a brand company into a *belief* company—one that could create positive social and environmental change. Under Jeffrey's tenure Timberland launched the social enterprise group within the company, became one of the first companies to give employees forty hours of paid leave to volunteer in their communities by way of its Path of Service program, and sponsored a companywide day of community service—Serv-a-Palooza—which has since become an annual worldwide event. The company's latest move was to "nutritionally label" the company's products, showing how much energy went into their manufacture.

If you look at Timberland's corporate timeline, you can see a clear inflection point at which the company changed from a traditional organization with a business mission to a new kind of organization with a business mission *and* a social mission. This inflection point occurred when the company began its partnership with City Year in 1989. Although the benefits of this partnership mostly flowed in one direction at the start—from Timberland to City Year—the benefits soon flowed from City Year to Timberland as well, influencing the Swartz family and helping enable the company's transition into a belief company. It's no accident that Timberland landed on *Fortune* magazine's 100 Best Places to Work For in 1997—a list it has been on every year since—and on *Working Mother* magazine's list of 100 Best Companies for Working Mothers in 2004.

If you don't yet have a strategic partnership with an NGO or nonprofit to support your CSR strategy, you may find that one is in your future. However, not just any partner will do, and there's a right way and a wrong way to develop and nurture your partnerships. Here are some tips for finding the right strategic partnership—and developing the kind of long-term relationship that will be good for both you and your partner:

- Select compatible partners that fit your mission.
- Come up with shared goals and objectives that are clear and concrete.
- Minimize the number of partnerships.
- Make a long-term commitment.
- Involve employees, customers, and suppliers in the selection process.
- Recognize that both partners, not just the corporation, bring strengths to the partnership.

- Develop a partnership management team.
- Communicate openly, honestly, and frequently.
- Communicate and market the partnership to stakeholders.
- Integrate the partnership into your business.
- Brand the partnership.
- Be strategic in your planning.

Partner with Other Companies Too

In April 2008 I led a symposium for Haitian business leaders on CSR. Because the challenges in Haiti are dire, the government is weak, and the aid society operates in the old-school method of philanthropy, the business sector, in order to thrive, has a critical role in society.

At the end of the first day, I asked some of the Haitian business leaders to stand up and speak about what their companies were doing in the CSR programs. Of the business leaders who spoke, about 90 percent of the programs were focused on education, which is abysmal in this country with a literacy rate of less than 50 percent of the population.[46] One leader would talk about physically building schools, while another would speak about a teacher-training program, and yet another would describe a computer-donation program. Yet none of these programs were aimed at the same parts of the country, the same locations, or even the same schools, so the impact was minimal.

In Haiti, as in every other part of the world, companies are not in the habit of speaking to one another, let alone working with one another. We have got to start reversing this trend and work in collaboration on our chosen social and environmental issues. You do not need to work with your fiercest competitor within your industry, but you can reach out across industries to other players who are working on the same issues, in the way Product Red has done. Imagine how much could be accomplished if HP joined Dove in developing self-esteem in young girls and women by teaching technical skills, and if Barclays joined to provide financial literacy training, and Nike joined to get more girls into sports. How much faster and more sustainably could we raise the self-esteem rates in women?

The Road Ahead

Consumer expectations for CSR are increasing. Companies have more opportunities to communicate and brand their CSR efforts and to involve their customers more deeply in the product experience. It used to be that consumers would say to businesses, "It's okay—just tell me what you're doing." Then consumers started saying, "Hey, you're telling us what you're doing, but now show us some data—show us proof that this is working." Now consumers, particularly members of the Millennial generation, are at a new stage where they are saying, "Involve us. We're beyond the tell-us stage, we're beyond the show-us stage, we want to be involved. We too want to take action."

This desire to be involved is why Whirlpool's partnership with Habitat for Humanity works so well. Whirlpool allows employees to volunteer in this program, and it also encourages its customers (and optimistically its suppliers) to join with them. Levi Strauss did the same thing with its 501 Day, in partnership with VolunteerMatch, when it said, "Not only are we out in the community volunteering on May 1, but we invite our customers to come out and join us." Customers are increasingly interested in taking action, and they are affiliating with companies that give them the opportunity to do just that.

Sparking a dialogue is a critical part of this entire process. One of the reasons the Dove campaign has been so successful is that it created water-cooler buzz. And with each new iteration of the campaign—such as a "pro-age" campaign aimed at women over fifty—an entirely new round of buzz is created. Oprah had Dove on numerous times, including appearances for the pro-age campaign. The campaign showed women over fifty in their bras and underwear, and Oprah had the women who posed for that campaign on her show.

That's the sort of PR that trumps traditional advertising hands down, and that costs far less. And there are blogs on the Dove Web site, so after you watch one of the company's compelling videos, you can blog about how it made you feel, or about your experiences with some of the things that the little girls are talking about. It's gone viral on YouTube, and it's sparking a huge amount of dialogue and consumer connectivity.

Many businesses are focusing on innovation, which is a buzzword today. There are significant opportunities for companies to link their CSR strategies to innovation, a linkage that can help them do business differently and rise above the noise. GE is doing a great job of that with Ecomagination, because it is saying that by pushing its products to be more energy efficient, it's developing more innovative products.

Setting clear-cut, measurable CSR goals is critical, and Wal-Mart has done a fantastic job of this. It's easy to criticize Wal-Mart and to assume that the company is just doing this just for positive PR, but it has done far more in its CSR strategy than many companies. It has set tangible, clear-cut goals such as moving to zero waste by 2015. As it reports its results moving toward that goal, it is showing that it is being authentic, despite what some people will say.

To close this book, I would like you to consider for a moment one of my favorite quotations, by Edmund Burke:

> The only thing necessary for the triumph of evil is for good men and women to do nothing.

Now that you've finished reading this book, you know how to develop an integrated CSR strategy, and you know how to turn it into a brand, communicate it, and tell your CSR story. As you reflect on what you have learned, I ask you just one thing: *please don't do nothing.*

Acknowledgments

As the plane began its descent into Port-au-Prince, Haiti, I could see from my window a sprawling mass of ramshackle shanties that stretched as far as the eye could see. I was reminded of something that Jeffrey Sachs said once to an audience of corporate CEOs: "If you think it's bad being exploited by a multinational corporation, try being ignored by one."

I would like to sincerely recognize the many committed companies with whom I have worked, as a speaker, consultant, and partner. These companies understand this subtle message from Jeffery Sachs, and they aren't ignoring either their core business objectives or their ability to use their vast power and resources to address our world's intractable social and environmental issues. The people in these companies are crusaders as they try each day to redefine the everyday way of doing business. They are the smart, committed, passionate, and compassionate business folks in companies like McDonald's, Hewlett-Packard, Ernst & Young, Gap, eBay, Triage Consulting Group, Brown-Forman, Driscoll Strawberry Associates, Whole Foods Market, Wal-Mart, Levi Strauss & Company, and Dow Chemical. Sometimes they have the support and leadership from their senior management; often they press forward without it. Sometimes they have the answers; often they make them up as they pioneer along. Sometimes they receive praise for their work; often they are criticized and told it is simultaneously unreasonable and not enough. Sometimes they get burned out; often they press forward to create change from within anyway. Without doers like these, I could not teach, research, work, or write about corporate social responsibility—all of which are part of my passion, my true calling in life.

I am indebted to the countless students I have taught in undergraduate, MBA, executive education, and corporate classrooms in California, Michigan, North Carolina, Ireland, France, and Haiti. These students take my concepts and ideas, make them better, and execute them in their companies. They energize me and keep me going with their stories, reports, e-mails, and phone calls. From time to time, I encounter my own roadblocks, both personal and professional, which knock me down for a spell. They have no idea how much they sustain me throughout these times.

I am honored to have studied and learned under Professor Stuart Hart during my graduate career, and I am glad I listened to him when he urged me to get out of my comfort zone and develop a new MBA course in CSR. That course was rejected twice by the faculty curriculum committee before they finally *let* me teach it. The class filled during the first day of student enrollment, and CSR classes have been filling ever since.

I am most thankful to Johanna Vondeling and Jeevan Sivasbramdnian at Berrett-Koehler, who approached me before I even knew where the bathrooms were at Berkeley and who remained calm yet persistent even though I threw every excuse in the book at them and delayed and delayed. They took a real chance on me. I am indebted to Peter Economy, who ultimately made the writing process collaborative, collegial, and connected—three things that I need in order to thrive in work. He made this book actually come to life.

I am thankful for my parents, for making me stubborn, competitive, and idealistic enough to fight harder when the inevitable naysayers said no and proudly recited why corporate social responsibility could and would not work.

And finally I am grateful to my family, who support, feed, and understand my passion and allow me to persevere and succeed—and now even join me in it.

I truly am one of the lucky ones who found my passion in my life's work and have been able to make an impact through it.

Notes

1. Alexander Wolff, "Going, Going Green," *Sports Illustrated*, March 6, 2007.

2. Simon Zadek, *The Civil Corporation: The New Economy of Corporate Citizenship* (Sterling, VA: Earthscan, 2001).

3. General Electric, *2007 Ecomagination Report*, Ecomagination.com, http://ge.ecomagination.com/site/downloads/news/2007ecoreport.pdf.

4. George Pohle and Jeff Hittner, *Attaining Sustainable Growth through Corporate Social Responsibility* (IBM Institute for Business Value, February 2008), p. 3, http://www-935.ibm.com/services/us/index.wss/ibvstudy/gbs/a1029293?cntxt=a1000074.

5. Michael E. Porter and Mark R. Kramer, "Strategy and Society: The Link between Competitive Advantage and Corporate Social Responsibility," *Harvard Business Review*, December 2006, p. 1.

6. Harry Hurt III, "The Green 11," *Condé Nast Portfolio*, March 2008.

7. Harry Hurt III, "The Toxic Ten," *Condé Nast Portfolio*, March 2008.

8. Edelman, *2006 Annual Edelman Trust Barometer*, http://www.edelman.com/trust/2008/prior/2006/FullSupplement_final.pdf.

9. Bob Willard, *The Next Sustainability Wave: Building Boardroom Buy-In* (Gabriola Island, BC: New Society Publishers, 2005).

10. Ronald Alsop, "How Boss's Deeds Buff a Firm's Reputation," *Wall Street Journal*, January 31, 2007, http://online.wsj.com/public/article/

SB117019715069692873-92u520ldt3ZTY_ZFX442W76FnfI_20080131.html
?mod=tff_main_tff_top.

11. Ibid.

12. Graham Page and Helen Fearn, "Corporate Reputation: What Do Customers Really Care About?" *Journal of Advertising Research,* September 2005.

13. Great Place to Work Institute, "Enhancing the Workplace Brings in Results," http://www.greatplacetowork.com/great/results.php.

14. Russell Investment Group and Great Place to Work Institute, "Fortune '100 Best' vs. Stock Market 1998–2006," http://www .greatplacetowork.com/great/graphs.php.

15. Faith Popcorn, *The Popcorn Report: Revolutionary Trend Predictions for Marketing in the 1990s* (London: Arrow Books, 1992); Cone, *2004 Corporate Citizenship Study,* http://www.coneinc.com.

16. Ford Motor Company, "Warriors in Pink Mustang: Ford Doubles Contribution to Susan G. Komen Foundation for the Cure," Ford Motor Company Global Auto Shows, http://autoshows.ford.com/226/2008/03/19/warriors-pink-mustang-ford/.

17. Breast cancer, *MayoClinic.com,* http://www.mayoclinic.com/health/breast-cancer/DS00328 (accessed June 23, 2008; Breast cancer, *Wikipedia,* http://en.wikipedia.org/wiki/Breast_cancer (accessed June 23, 2008).

18. Ford Motor Company, *2007 Annual Report,* p. 6

19. Carolyn J. Simmons and Karen Becker-Olsen, "Fortifying or Diluting Equity via Association: The Case of Sponsorship," *Journal of Marketing,* October 2006.

20. Jack Neff, "In Dove Ads, Normal Is the New Beautiful," *Advertising Age,* September 27, 2004.

21. The Web site is www.campaignforrealbeauty.com.

22. The Web site is www.pedigree.com.

23. Jennifer Aaker, presentation at Google.

24. The Web site is www.theaxeeffect.com.

25. Axe, "What Will Axe's Improved Fragrance Do for Me?" http://www.theaxeeffect.com/axeshowergel.html?utm_source=google&utm_medium=sem&utm_content=branded&utm_campaign=bass (accessed April 24, 2008; page now discontinued).

26. Wyatt Buchanan, "S.F. Expected to Pass Law on Nutrition Disclosure," *San Francisco Chronicle,* February 29, 2008.

27. The Web site is www.methodhome.com.

28. The Web site is www.volunteermatch.org.

29. The Web site is www.levi.com.

30. Starbucks, "Environmental Mission Statement," http://www
.starbucks.com/aboutus/environment.asp.

31. The Web site is www.starbucks.com.

32. Starbucks, *Corporate Social Responsibility: Fiscal 2006 Annual
Report*, 2006, http://www.starbucks.com/aboutus/csr.asp.

33. "Fortune 500, 2007," CNNMoney.com, http://money.cnn.com/
magazines/fortune/fortune500/2007/full_list/201_300.html.

34. Matt Richtel, "Going to the Company Elders for Help," *New York
Times*, March 10, 2008.

35. Wal-Mart, "Sustainability Progress Report," Wal-Mart, http://
walmartstores.com/Sustainability/7951.aspx.(Accessed April 25, 2008.)

36. Jim Carlton, "Despite Marketing, Wal-Mart Declares: 'We Are Not
Green,'" *Wall Street Journal*, March 14, 2008, p. B6.

37. Fleishman-Hillard and National Consumers League, *Rethinking
Corporate Social Responsibility*, CSR Survey 07, http://www.csrresults.com/;
Globescan, "Corporate Social Responsibility Monitor," http://www.globescan
.com/csrm_overview.htm.

38. "Fortune 500, 2007."

39. GreenBiz Staff, "GE Launches Program to Develop Environmental
Technologies," *Greenbiz.com*, May 12, 2005, http://www.greenbiz.com/news/
2005/05/12/ge-launches-program-develop-environmental-technologies.

40. General Electric, *2007 Ecomagination Report*.

41. Michael Specter, "Big Foot," *New Yorker*, February 25, 2008, http://
www.newyorker.com/reporting/2008/02/25/080225fa_fact_specter
?currentPage=all.

42. Amy Cortese, "Business: They Care about the World (and They Shop,
Too)," *New York Times*, July 20, 2003.

43. Natural Marketing Institute, "Understanding the LOHAS Market
Report," http://www.nmisolutions.com/r_lohas.html.

44. Environics International, *CSR Monitor*, 2005; Hill & Knowlton/Harris
Interactive, *Corporate Citizen Watch*, 2001; Cone, *Cause Evolution Study*,
2007.

45. Edelman, *2006 Annual Edelman Trust Barometer*, http://www
.edelman.com/trust/2008/prior/2006/FullSupplement_final.pdf.

46. IMF country report No 07/293: Haiti 2007 Article IV Consultation.
Aaker, Jennifer, 55

Index

About the Author

Kellie A. McElhaney is the John C. Whitehead Adjunct Professor of Corporate Responsibility at the Haas School of Business at the University of California, Berkeley. She is the founding director and co-faculty director of the Center for Responsible Business, which has helped make corporate responsibility one of the core competencies and competitive advantages of the Haas School. The *Wall Street Journal* ranked Haas as the number two business school in the country for corporate social responsibility in 2006 and 2007, and the *Financial Times* rated Haas as the number one school in the world in 2008! She teaches courses on strategic corporate social responsibility, and the courses include in-depth, experiential consulting engagements with companies on high-visibility strategic CSR challenges.

Kellie was named a Faculty Pioneer for leading institutional change by the Aspen Institute, which hailed her as one of the world's leading thinkers on strategic CSR. She focuses her research in three areas: analyzing and developing companies' CSR strategies and how they align with core business objectives, core competencies, and business value; exploring the linkage between gender and CSR and using CSR as a hook to reengage women with business as employees, consumers, entrepreneurs, and investors; and examining the business value and opportunities in branding, communication, and CSR.

Kellie consults to several Fortune 500 companies in developing integrated CSR strategy. Her client list includes Hewlett-Packard, Gap, eBay, McDonald's, Ernst & Young, Driscoll Strawberry Associates, Nokia, Navigant International, VolunteerMatch, Ford Motor Company, Ulster Bank, Blue Cross and Blue Shield, and Catholic Healthcare West. A highly engaging and motivational public speaker in the area of CSR, she has keynoted at major conferences, leadership summits, and corporate events.

Her consulting expertise includes the following areas:

- Assessing current CSR initiatives and identifying gaps, strengths, opportunities, and risks
- Developing and integrating CSR strategy with a company's core business objectives and core competencies to produce financial and social or environmental returns
- Benchmarking of peer sectors, industries for good practices, industry leaders, and company placement among peers
- Facilitating and leading global corporate stakeholder dialogues, both internally and externally
- Developing and teaching in-house CSR education programs for company leaders, managers, and senior executives
- Analyzing, assessing, and improving CSR branding, communication, reporting, and measurement
- Coaching and advising corporate leaders who are trying to introduce, develop, or integrate CSR strategy and/or product/service offerings within their companies

Kellie helped found and serves on the board of directors of Foundation Île à Vache, which supports infrastructural and economic development on the island in southern Haiti. She is also on the management team of the Encircle Foundation, which fosters corporate support of the Millennium Development Goals by launching enterprise solutions to poverty, and is on the boards of Net Impact and VolunteerMatch. She lives in the Oakland hills in California. She enjoys photography, yoga, good wine, running, and has even tried surfing.

About Berrett-Koehler Publishers

Berrett-Koehler is an independent publisher dedicated to an ambitious mission: Creating a World That Works for All.

We believe that to truly create a better world, action is needed at all levels—individual, organizational, and societal. At the individual level, our publications help people align their lives with their values and with their aspirations for a better world. At the organizational level, our publications promote progressive leadership and management practices, socially responsible approaches to business, and humane and effective organizations. At the societal level, our publications advance social and economic justice, shared prosperity, sustainability, and new solutions to national and global issues.

A major theme of our publications is "Opening Up New Space." They challenge conventional thinking, introduce new ideas, and foster positive change. Their common quest is changing the underlying beliefs, mindsets, institutions, and structures that keep generating the same cycles of problems, no matter who our leaders are or what improvement programs we adopt.

We strive to practice what we preach—to operate our publishing company in line with the ideas in our books. At the core of our approach is *stewardship*, which we define as a deep sense of responsibility to administer the company for the benefit of all of our "stakeholder" groups: authors, customers, employees, investors, service providers, and the communities and environment around us.

We are grateful to the thousands of readers, authors, and other friends of the company who consider themselves to be part of the "BK Community." We hope that you, too, will join us in our mission.

Be Connected

Visit Our Website

Go to www.bkconnection.com to read exclusive previews and excerpts of new books, find detailed information on all Berrett-Koehler titles and authors, browse subject-area libraries of books, and get special discounts.

Subscribe to Our Free E-Newsletter

Be the first to hear about new publications, special discount offers, exclusive articles, news about bestsellers, and more! Get on the list for our free e-newsletter by going to www.bkconnection.com.

Get Quantity Discounts

Berrett-Koehler books are available at quantity discounts for orders of ten or more copies. Please call us toll-free at (800) 929-2929 or email us at bkp.orders@aidcvt.com.

Host a Reading Group

For tips on how to form and carry on a book reading group in your workplace or community, see our website at www.bkconnection.com.

Join the BK Community

Thousands of readers of our books have become part of the "BK Community" by participating in events featuring our authors, reviewing draft manuscripts of forthcoming books, spreading the word about their favorite books, and supporting our publishing program in other ways. If you would like to join the BK Community, please contact us at bkcommunity@bkpub.com.